# OFF THE BEATEN PATH

# OFF THE BEATEN PATH

## A Hiking Guide
## to
## Vancouver's North Shore

### EXPANDED SECOND EDITION

## Norman D. Watt

HARBOUR PUBLISHING

**Harbour Publishing Co. Ltd.**
P.O. Box 219, Madeira Park, BC, V0N 2H0
www.harbourpublishing.com

Cover photograph of hikers on
Juniper Point Trail by David Nunuk
Edited by Margaret Tessman
Maps by John Lightfoot
Printed and bound in Canada

Canada Council    Conseil des Arts
for the Arts      du Canada

BRITISH
COLUMBIA
ARTS COUNCIL
Supported by the Province of British Columbia

Harbour Publishing acknowledges financial support from the
Government of Canada through the Book Publishing Industry
Development Program and the Canada Council for the Arts,
and from the Province of British Columbia through the BC Arts
Council and the Book Publishing Tax Credit.

*Caution:* Every effort has been made to ensure the reader's aware-
ness of the hazards and level of expertise involved in the activities
in this book, but your own safety is ultimately up to you. The
author and publisher take no responsibility for loss or injury
incurred by anyone using this book.

Cataloguing data available from Library and Archives Canada
ISBN 978-1-55017-636-0 (paper)
ISBN 978-1-55017-638-4 (ebook)

*This book is dedicated to my son, Geoffrey, and daughter, Stephanie, who both grew up on the North Shore of Metro Vancouver.
I hope this book will help them get as much enjoyment as I have had, exploring the great outdoors right here in our own backyard.*

# Contents

Introduction   11

## WEST VANCOUVER

**1** ► Lighthouse Park   17
**2** ► Seaview Walk   21
**3** ► Whyte Lake   25
**4** ► Cypress Falls Park to Nelson Canyon Park   29
**5** ► Eagle Bluff and Black Mountain   34
**6** ► St. Mark's Summit   38
**7** ► Mount Strachan   42
**8** ► Hollyburn Peak   47
**9** ► Hollyburn Cabin Country   51
**10** ► Hollyburn Lakes Circuit   55
**11** ► Trans Canada Trail/Millstream Trail Loop   59
**12** ► The Old Brewis Trail   63
**13** ► Upper Brothers Creek   67
**14** ► Brothers Creek/Ballantree Park   71
**15** ► Ballantree Park from Cleveland Dam   76
**16** ► Capilano Pacific Trail   80

## BADEN-POWELL TRAIL

Introduction   84
**17** ► Baden-Powell #1, Western End to Cypress Bowl   86
**18** ► Baden-Powell #2, Cypress Bowl to Cleveland Dam   92
**19** ► Baden-Powell #3, Grouse Mountain to Lynn Canyon   98
**20** ► Baden-Powell #4, Lynn Canyon to Deep Cove   103

## NORTH VANCOUVER

**21** ▸ Capilano Canyon 108

**22** ▸ Grouse Mountain–Lower Fromme Round Trip 113

**23** ▸ Mount Fromme 118

**24** ▸ St. Marys/Dempsey/Baden-Powell Loop 123

**25** ▸ Norvan Falls 128

**26** ▸ Lynn Peak and Lynn Loop 133

**27** ▸ Lynn Creek and Rice Lake 138

**28** ▸ Richard Juryn Trail/Old Lillooet Trail 142

**29** ▸ Upper Fisherman's Trail 146

**30** ▸ Seymour–Lynn Canyon Round Trip 151

**31** ▸ Lower Seymour Conservation Reserve 155

**32** ▸ Mushroom Parking Lot 160

**33** ▸ The TNT Trail 164

**34** ▸ Bridle Path Ramble 168

**35** ▸ Mount Seymour Vancouver Picnic Area 172

**36** ▸ Dinkey Peak and Dog Mountain 176

**37** ▸ Mystery Lake and Mystery Peak 180

**38** ▸ Goldie and Flower Lakes 184

**39** ▸ Quarry Rock 188

## ADDENDUM

Two Pemberton Area Hikes—
   Marriott Lake and Rohr Lake 193


Acknowledgements 197

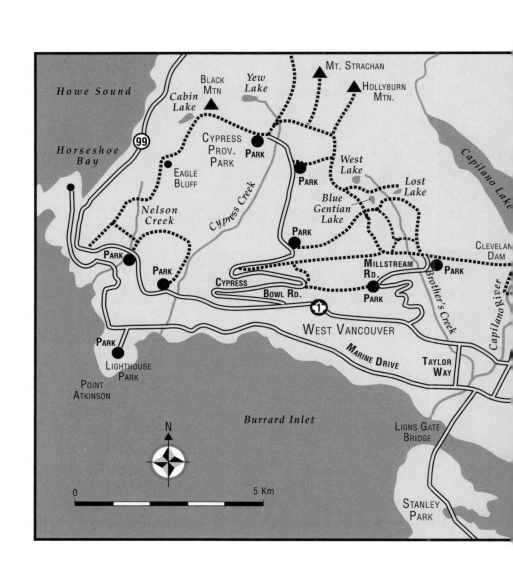

Howe Sound

Horseshoe
Bay

**99**

Cabin
Lake

Black
Mtn

Yew
Lake

Mt. Strachan

Hollyburn
Mtn.

Capilano Lake

Eagle
Bluff

Cypress
Prov.
Park

Park

West
Lake

Lost
Lake

Nelson
Creek

Cypress Creek

Blue
Gentian
Lake

Cleveland
Dam

Park

Park

Park

Park

Cypress

Bowl Rd.

Millstream
Rd.

Park

Brother's Creek

Park

Capilano River

**1**

West Vancouver

Park

Lighthouse
Park

Marine Drive

Taylor
Way

Point
Atkinson

Burrard Inlet

Lions Gate
Bridge

N

0                    5 Km

Stanley
Park

# INTRODUCTION

The genesis of this book was back in January 2008, when I first came up with the idea of writing descriptions of some North and West Vancouver hiking trails that I had come to know so well over a period of years. I approached the local newspapers with the idea of a hiking column featuring some of this area's lesser-known trails. The *North Shore News* agreed to run the column during July and August 2008 and "Off the Beaten Path" was born.

Expanding these initial articles and adding enough new ones to make a book seemed to be a logical next step. I began the book project in fall 2008, along with writing new articles for the summer 2009 hiking column, which was also carried by the *North Shore News*. The first edition of this book, published in 2010, consisted of 21 hike descriptions from those newspaper columns, in addition to another 10 new ones not previously published in the newspaper.

This second, expanded edition adds 8 new hikes, selected to appeal to hikers of varying interests and abilities. The more ambitious ones include some of the "high points" of the North Shore: Mount Strachan, Grouse Mountain, Mount Fromme and Lynn Peak. It also updates all of the original 31 hikes to reflect changes in trailhead access, signage, trail descriptions and, in some cases, to include winter snow hiking information or additional photographs.

The book's focus is on hiking trails through the wilderness of the North Shore forests of Metro Vancouver. As its title implies, this book is unique in that for the most part, these are lesser-known but interesting trails that people may not have seen before in other hiking books. Many of them feature sites of local historical interest, such as early 1900s' logging, homesteading or sporting activities, which are not often found in other hiking books. The level of detail, including thorough trail descriptions and approximate walking times throughout the hikes, also makes this book a distinctive and invaluable resource for the hiker.

There is much here to offer the seasoned outdoor adventurer as well as the casual hiker. With a total of 39 North Shore hikes (18 West Vancouver and 21 North Vancouver), this is the most comprehensive collection of North Shore hiking trails to be found in any hiking book. The remarkable, 48-kilometre (30-mile) Baden-Powell Trail that stretches from one end of the North Shore to the other has its own complete section, divided into four manageable segments. Portions of the Baden-Powell Trail are also included in many of the other hikes in the West Vancouver and North Vancouver sections.

There is no particular logic to the order of the hikes in this book, other than they are sequenced roughly west to east in each of the three sections.

# Trail Information

This book is intended for hikers of all ability levels. A range of estimated timings is provided for each hike to allow for differences in individual walking pace, depending on energy and fitness levels. While the hike could be completed in less time than the low end of the range, the upper end is intended to be generous enough to provide adequate time for most hikers. Most of these hikes are between two and four hours, although there are a few in the five- to six-hour range. The durations noted do not include time for a lunch stop, unless otherwise specified.

Elevation gains are generally the difference between the hike's lowest point (not necessarily the trailhead) and its highest point. They can be used as a good measure of a hike's suitability for you, although they are not cumulative! The 1:50,000 series of federal government topographical maps, available at International Travel Maps and Books, 12300 Bridgeport Road in Richmond

(604-273-1400 or itmb.ca), or at Mountain Equipment Co-op (MEC), 212 Brooksbank Avenue in North Vancouver (604-990-4417 or mec.ca), may also be helpful to illustrate the area's topography, although these maps do not include the hiking trails. The 1:20,000 North Shore Trail Map from Trail Ventures BC, issued in 2012 and also available from MEC, provides a very useful, comprehensive guide to all of the North Shore trails.

While all but three of these hikes are dog-friendly, many of them have signs posted requiring dogs to be on-leash in certain areas.

The season designations are intended to be a general guide to the most appropriate time of year for hiking the trails. You should, however, take into account the effect of current weather conditions. For example, heavy rainfall can turn some trails into creek beds, while unusually heavy snowfall, such as that experienced in the winter of 2008–09, can make even some lower elevation trails difficult to navigate until much later in the spring than usual. High winds at any time of year can bring down trees that will block a trail for extended periods of time.

Although every effort has been made to ensure that these hike descriptions are accurate at time of writing, trails are often altered from one year to the next for various reasons. All of the hikes in this book have been travelled between 2011 and 2013, with over 30 of them travelled between January and October 2013. Also, the West Vancouver hike descriptions do reflect the changes made to routes and trailheads for the 2009 Highway 1/99 Eagleridge Bypass project and the 2010 Olympics-related construction on Cypress Mountain.

# Transportation

Most of these hikes are accessible by public transit. Translink's customer information number is 604-953-3333. Their website, translink.ca, provides a Trip Planner, where you can enter your departure point and destination to get bus schedule and route information, including a map. Where applicable I have noted the hikes where private vehicle transportation is required.

# Hiking Safety

Hiking does involve an element of risk, and you should take the appropriate steps to ensure your own safety. In addition to your fitness and experience levels, consider external factors such as mountain conditions (wet, slippery, icy trails) and the weather (heat, fog, heavy rainfall, snow, etc.). Even familiar trails look very different under a blanket of snow, and it is easy to go astray when you cannot see the path beneath your feet.

Many of the trails in this book are also used by mountain bikers. Be alert for them coming downhill toward you, particularly on steep trails where it may be difficult for them to stop.

While bear encounters on these trails are not commonplace, they can and do occur. Many hikers, particularly when travelling alone, use bear bells to alert any nearby bears of their presence. Bear bells are inexpensive and are available from MEC.

Note the number of daylight hours left before embarking on any hike, and leave yourselves a generous amount of daylight time, particularly if you are unfamiliar with the area. Lack of light is the single most common cause of overdue hiker calls to North Shore Rescue.

The following safety information is provided courtesy of North Shore Rescue. It is summarized with permission from its website, northshorerescue.com/education, where additional detail is available.

## What to Bring—The Ten Essentials

Even the best weather can change rapidly, and even the widest trail can be lost. It pays to take a little extra with you, just in case. North Shore Rescue recommends taking the following:

1. Flashlight or a headlamp with extra batteries and light bulb. Bring a small LED light as emergency backup.

2. Whistle (such as the Fox 40 whistle with a lanyard).

3. Matches (waterproof or in plastic bag) or lighter.

4. Extra clothes: hat or toque, gloves or mittens, fleece jacket, Gore-Tex jacket, polypro underwear, good quality hiking socks and Gore-Tex overpants.

5. Pocketknife with quality cutting blade.

6. Large orange plastic bag and thermal tarp.

7. Water (Gatorade crystals recommended) and food (high-energy food bars).

8. First-aid kit: should include CPR pocket mask, SAM splint, bulk dressings, protective gloves, bandages, scissors and blister dressings.

9. Navigation aids: good-quality compass with built-in declination adjustment, and both topographical and interpretive maps. Also a GPS unit, as an adjunct to compass and map.

10. Communication tools: a fully charged cellphone with extra batteries. Also consider purchasing a two-way family radio system called FRS. A personal locator beacon such as a SPOT is also recommended.

## Ways to Avoid Becoming Lost and What to Do if You Do Become Lost

If you get lost today, will anyone know? Are you prepared?

• Leave a message with a friend. A note, left with a responsible person, explains your destination, the route you are taking, who is with you and your return time.

• Always carry the 10 essentials. Be ready to stay out overnight in a survival situation. Carry extra clothing, survival gear and be mentally prepared to endure the night out.

• Never hike alone. Hike with a group and keep together. If a person becomes separated by going ahead or falling behind, that person is more likely to become lost.

• Be physically prepared and fit enough to enjoy your chosen hike. Stick to a turnaround time and leave enough time to get home without causing people to worry about you. Take the proper equipment and have a trip plan.

• Do not panic. Maintain a positive mental attitude if you become lost. Being lost is not dangerous if you are prepared.

• Stay where you are. People who go on after becoming lost usually get farther from the trail and farther from people who are looking for them. Help will come.

• Do not go "downhill." On the North Shore, going downhill often leads to dangerous natural drainages. These drainages have the common features of very thick bush, steep cliffs and waterfalls.

• Use signalling devices. Blowing a whistle, lighting a fire and staying visible will help searchers find you. Help people trying to find you, even if you feel embarrassed or afraid. Animals will not be attracted to your signals.

• Build or seek shelter. Protect yourself from the elements. Be as comfortable as possible, but when it is light make sure you are visible to searchers in helicopters or planes.

It could happen to you. Bad weather, early darkness or an unexpected injury can turn an easy hike into an extended crisis. By being prepared you will enjoy your trip in the backcountry regardless of what nature throws at you.

The lighthouse at Point Atkinson in Lighthouse Park.

# WEST VANCOUVER
## 1 ▸ Lighthouse Park

**Elevation gain:** minimal
**High point:** 115 metres (380 feet)
**Season:** Year-round
**Topographical map:** North Vancouver 92G06
**Hiking time:** 2 to 2½ hours
Dog-friendly

Here is a year-round, energetic outing to a National Historic Site with rewarding views across both Burrard Inlet and Howe Sound as you roam through Metro Vancouver's last stand of rugged, old-growth rainforest. You take a clockwise circuit of the park, starting with a trek to its high point on the quieter, less-visited east side, followed by some fine viewpoints on the better-known south and west coastal sides. Do exercise caution on the park's large rock outcroppings such as the summit and the rocky waterfront bluffs, as they can be quite slippery when wet.

From the north end of the Lions Gate Bridge, go west along Marine Drive in West Vancouver for not quite 10 kilometres (6 miles). Just past a fire hall on your right, go up a short rise in the road and turn left onto Beacon Lane, marked by a wooden

"Lighthouse Park" sign. Follow Beacon Lane south to the parking lot.

Begin at the information kiosk at the top of the parking lot, where there is a large map of the park trails, as well as helpful handout maps. Walk past the yellow gate and turn left at the sign-posted Salal Loop Trail. This trail is somewhat rocky and rooty, and can be slippery when wet. Follow it uphill, staying to the right at the next three junctions. At the second fire hydrant, 5 to 10 minutes from the start, turn right for a short scramble up a side trail leading you to the park's summit. Here you have a southerly viewpoint, albeit rather obstructed due to the surrounding trees.

Coming down from the summit, go right at the fire hydrant to continue east and downhill on the Summit Trail. This is a fairly rough trail, but easy to follow. Stay to the right at the next three junctions. About 10 minutes from the summit, you reach a

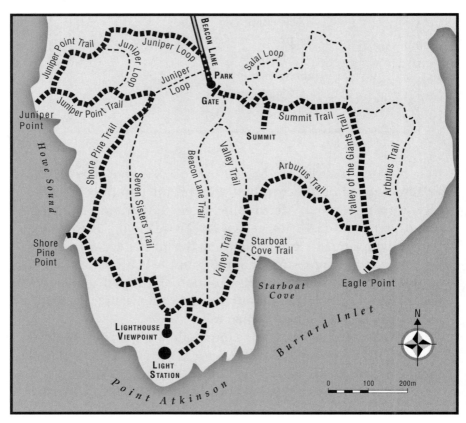

signposted junction where the Arbutus Trail goes left, but you go right on the aptly named Valley of the Giants Trail. This trail is a streambed during periods of heavy rainfall, but it does reward you with views of magnificent western red cedar, western hemlock and Douglas fir, some of which are over 60 metres (200 feet) tall and around 500 years old.

After another 10 minutes or so you reach another signposted junction with the Arbutus Trail. Continue straight ahead and out onto the rocky bluffs of Eagle Point. Here, amidst some hardy arbutus and pine, you are treated to 180-degree views of the North Shore, Lions Gate Bridge, Stanley Park, Vancouver and Point Grey.

Returning to the main trail again, go left on the Arbutus Trail, following it uphill then downhill, but generally west to its junction with the Valley Trail. If you are short of time you could turn right here to return directly to the parking lot.

Otherwise, go left to follow the Valley Trail south, then left again at the signposted junction for Starboat Cove. A comfortable bench on the bluff overlooking the water provides another fine southerly viewpoint. Return to the Valley Trail and continue west to the cluster of buildings at Point Atkinson, named after a friend by Captain George Vancouver in 1792.

Looking northwest from Juniper Point.

If the gate is open, you can walk down for a closer look at the lighthouse itself. The first lighthouse was built here in 1874. Seven years later the federal government spared the surrounding forest by reserving 75 hectares (185 acres) of land as a dark backdrop for the lighthouse beacon. You can also take in the interpretive centre at Phyl Munday Nature House, open Sundays from 2:00 to 4:00 p.m. Volunteers maintain the centre, which is named in memory of Phyllis Munday (1894–1990), a renowned mountaineer, naturalist and Girl Guide leader.

From here you could return to the parking lot in 10 to 15 minutes by taking the Beacon Lane Trail north. Otherwise, continue west, following the "View" signs, to the nearby Lighthouse Viewpoint. Here you will find a historic cairn that names the past lighthouse keepers, and notes that the first white child born in West Vancouver (James Atkinson Woodward, in 1876) was the son of the first keeper, Edwin Woodward. The present lighthouse was built in 1912; it was designated a National Historic Site in 1994 and has been automated since 1996.

Continuing northwest on the Shore Pine Trail, you pass a junction with Seven Sisters Trail and another signed lookout point at lovely West Beach before coming to Shore Pine Point (a.k.a. Jack Pine Point on the large wooden sign) about 10 to 15 minutes from the lighthouse. Here you have a fine view over to Bowen Island and the Coast Range off to the north.

Continue north on the Shore Pine Trail, staying left at its junction with Seven Sisters Trail. About 50 metres (165 feet) ahead, you could return to the parking lot in 5 minutes by taking the Juniper Loop Trail to the right. Otherwise, stay left at each of the Juniper Loop Trail junctions to follow the Juniper Point Trail down to the large rocky bluff of Juniper Point, about 20 minutes from Shore Pine Point.

To return, take the Juniper Point Trail left up the sturdy wooden staircase, and go left at a large rock face to reach its signposted junction with the Juniper Loop Trail. From here either way will take you out, but the left route is a little shorter, returning you to the parking lot 10 to 15 minutes from Juniper Point.

# 2 ▶ Seaview Walk

**Elevation gain:** minimal
**High point:** 100 metres (330 feet)
**Season:** Year-round
**Topographical map:** North Vancouver 92G06
**Hiking time:** 1½ to 2½ hours
Dog-friendly

This pleasant, all-season jaunt along part of the Trans Canada Trail (TCT) is more of a walk than a hike, a perfect option if you are looking for something varied and interesting but not too long or strenuous. It takes you along West Vancouver's quiet Seaview Walk, with its panoramic marine views, then out to picturesque Horseshoe Bay. You can make an optional short side trip down to secluded Larson Bay Park, named after Peter Larson, who owned much of the surrounding land from 1902 to 1927.

From Highway 1 in West Vancouver, you reach the trailhead by taking Exit 4, then turning left onto Westport Road. Go straight through at the four-way stop and follow Westport Road for about 1½ kilometres (1 mile). Just after passing under the highway you see a Whyte Lake "P" for parking sign marking the small gravel parking area on the right-hand side.

Begin by walking past the yellow gate, along the winding gravel road and back under the highway. In less than 5 minutes you reach a signpost on part of the original Upper Levels Highway, which was completed in the late 1950s. Continuing straight ahead into the woods would take you north toward Whyte Lake (see hike #3), but you go left, now on the TCT, to cross Nelson Creek on the old highway bridge.

About 50 metres (165 feet) past the bridge, at a signposted trail junction, go down to your left on a curving gravel path, which joins the Seaview Walk in about 5 minutes. Coming up from the left is a short trail from Cranley Drive, another possible starting point for this hike (Cranley Drive joins Marine Drive just east of Eagle Harbour). You now go west along the scenic Seaview Walk, once the right-of-way of the former BC Railway prior to a tunnel being completed in 1973 (the tunnel entrance can be seen through the chain-link fence to your left).

In 10 to 15 minutes you are treated to views of Eagle Harbour and Eagle Island down to your left, Caulfeild Plateau off to the southeast and 1,094-metre (3,590-foot) Eagle Bluff (see hike #5) high up to the northeast. After strolling along for about 1½ kilometres (1 mile) and roughly 20 minutes you reach a yellow gate at Eagleridge Drive. Cross here and continue along the path, which drops down to follow Marine Drive for about 150 metres (500 feet) to a crosswalk at Orchill Road and the Gleneagles Golf Course. Here you have two choices: continuing to Horseshoe Bay or visiting Larson Bay Park.

For the latter option, follow Orchill Road, passing the parking area then the clubhouse on your left. About 100 metres (330 feet) past the clubhouse and just after the road crosses Larson Creek, go left to take a path along the right-hand side of the fairway. In about 50 metres (165 feet) you join a very pleasant, winding dirt trail alongside the creek. Cross the creek and continue down

Eagle Harbour from the Seaview Walk.

the trail, bypassing the old sets of steps on your left that would take you up toward Gleneagles Drive, until you reach small, quiet Larson Bay about 10 minutes from the clubhouse. After admiring the westerly views over to Bowen Island and nearby Passage Island, and perhaps enjoying a summer swim, retrace your steps back to where Orchill Road joins Marine Drive.

From here you could return to the Whyte Lake parking lot or, if time permits, carry on for another 15 to 20 minutes to visit Horseshoe Bay. If the latter, go left, following the Seaview Walk path along the back of the Gleneagles Community Centre, dirt bike/skateboard park and fire hall. Emerging onto Marine Drive you next pass the Lions Club day parking lot across the road on your right, then Gleneagles Ch'axáy Elementary School on your left before arriving at a roundabout where Marine Drive turns sharply right. Cross at the crosswalk then take the signposted steps down toward Horseshoe Bay, staying to your right at the first two trail junctions.

In Horseshoe Bay there are many options for food and drink, or you may just wish to relax in Horseshoe Bay Park itself. When you are ready to start back, the return trip to the Whyte Lake parking lot from Horseshoe Bay is 60 to 75 minutes.

# 3 ▶ Whyte Lake

**Elevation gain:** 190 metres (620 feet)
**High point:** 320 metres (1,050 feet)
**Season:** Most of the year
**Topographical map:** North Vancouver 92G06
**Hiking time:** 2 to 2½ hours
Dog-friendly

This quiet, interesting little trek follows the first few (easy) kilometres of the Knee Knackering North Shore Trail Run (KKNSTR) on your way to West Vancouver's rather secluded but very pretty Whyte Lake. It is also the recently improved access to the western end of the Baden-Powell (BP) Trail (see hike #17), with the completion of the new Highway 1/99 Eagleridge Bypass in early 2009. The hike follows the Trans Canada Trail (TCT) through Nelson Canyon Park via Nelson Creek, then goes along Whyte Creek over to Whyte Lake, with an optional loop around part of the BP on the way back.

From Highway 1 in West Vancouver, you reach the trailhead by taking Exit 4, then turning left onto Westport Road. Go straight through at the four-way stop and follow Westport Road for about 1½ kilometres (1 mile). Just after passing under the highway you see a Whyte Lake "P" for parking sign marking the small gravel parking area on the right-hand side.

On the south shore of Whyte Lake.

Begin by walking past the yellow gate, along the winding gravel road and back under the highway. In about 5 minutes you come to a TCT signpost, where you keep going straight ahead for Whyte Lake. After another couple of minutes turn right into the woods at a second TCT signpost. Following the winding uphill trail you soon hear Nelson Creek on your left. Nelson Creek was named after August Nelson, a local framer and planerman who had a mill site at Eagle Harbour in the 1890s.

About 15 to 20 minutes from the parking area, you leave the main trail by going down to your left at a signposted junction. (Continuing straight ahead could lead you along the TCT to Cypress Falls Park; see hike #4.) In about 5 minutes this meandering trail leads to the Nelson Creek crossing on a sturdy footbridge built in 2008 by West Vancouver's noted bridge builder Mark Kachaluba. This recently improved trail now heads west, following Whyte Creek on your left. Whyte Creek and Whyte Lake were named for Colonel Albert Whyte, an owner of the West Shore and Northern Land Company in the early 1900s. The company bought and developed land in the Horseshoe Bay and Whyte Cliff

City area, the latter renamed Whytecliff through the urging of Albert Whyte in 1914.

Shortly after taking a footbridge across Whyte Creek, and about 30 metres (100 feet) before reaching the first of three boardwalks across a marshy area, there is a short signposted trail off to your right. This path leads to the south shore of Whyte Lake, just past the foundation of an old log cabin. The lake, suitable for swimming, has a nice little wharf complete with a bench. Back on the main trail, and after the third boardwalk, you come to a signposted junction just below a unique, wooden, stable-door outhouse. Access to the BP Trail is to your left, but you follow the trail to your right, and in less than 5 minutes, watch for a small, unmarked trail that in another couple of minutes leads you down to the serene northwest side of Whyte Lake. In the early 1900s a water flume was built to carry logs (from a commercial logging operation on Black Mountain) from here down to Horseshoe Bay.

From here you can retrace your steps back to the junction with the main Whyte Creek trail. However, if you have an extra 30 to 40 minutes and don't mind a little elevation gain, you can do a side trip out to the BP instead, by leaving the lakeside and turning right on the trail that brought you there. This trail is not well marked, but is well-worn and quite easy to follow. You go straight ahead then left through salal bushes up a fairly steep slope then downhill to an unmarked junction with the BP in 15 minutes.

Turn left to go downhill on the BP, which is wide and rocky at this point. After another 10 to 15 minutes you reach a signposted junction with a trail branching off to the left. This is the trail back to Whyte Lake. You go up a fairly steep slope for a couple of minutes, then left and downhill to the junction where you originally turned off to get to the shoreline of the lake.

To return to the parking area, start back along the boardwalk, noticing Eagle Bluff, the goal of the next few (not so easy) kilometres of the KKNSTR and the BP, looming up to the north at 1,094 metres (3,590 feet) elevation. You first follow Whyte Creek east, then Nelson Creek south, reaching your car about 40 to 50 minutes from the Whyte Lake junction.

# 4 ▶ Cypress Falls Park to Nelson Canyon Park

**Elevation gain:** 250 metres (820 feet)
**High point:** 440 metres (1,440 feet)
**Season:** Most of the year
**Topographical map:** North Vancouver 92G06
**Hiking time:** 2 to 2½ hours
Dog-friendly

Here is a hike that introduces you to two of West Vancouver's lesser-known but quite charming parks: Cypress Falls Park, with its dramatic waterfalls; and Nelson Canyon Park, with its massive, second-growth Douglas firs and western red cedars. In between, a ramble along the Trans Canada Trail (TCT) makes this a satisfying outing almost any time of year. The hike starts in Cypress Falls Park and takes you along part of the TCT into Nelson Canyon Park. This is a one-way hike, so you may wish to leave a second car at the end to avoid a walk back along Westport Road.

From Highway 1 in West Vancouver you reach the trailhead by taking Exit 4, then turning right at the stop sign for Woodgreen Drive and right again at Woodgreen Place. Park in the upper parking area on your left just past the tennis courts.

To first leave a car at the other end, turn left from the Highway 1 exit onto Westport Road. Go straight through at the four-way stop and follow Westport Road for about 1½ kilometres (1 mile). Just after passing under the highway you see a Whyte Lake "P" for parking sign marking the small gravel parking area on the right-hand side. Then follow Westport Road back to Woodgreen Drive and Woodgreen Place.

Begin by going straight east across the clearing into the forest. Turn left and head gradually uphill on the wide dirt trail. In a couple of minutes take the trail down to your right and follow it uphill, being wary of some steep drop-offs on your right-hand side. In about 5 minutes you come to the impressive lower falls viewpoint.

Continue a little farther uphill until you reach a fence and warning sign, then make your way up to the left to return to the main trail. Go right and uphill for a few metres, then down

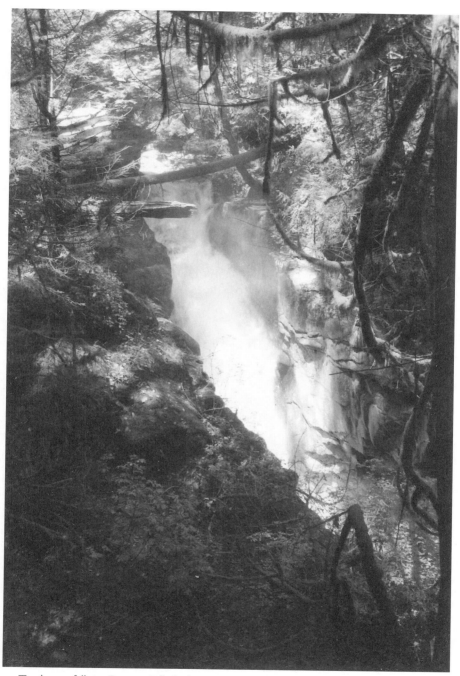

The lower falls in Cypress Falls Park.

to your right to a lookout over the waterfall. Follow this side trail up to a footbridge above the falls. Rather than cross the bridge, continue up the west side of Cypress Creek on the old, switch-backing dirt trail. This trail through some grand old Douglas firs is not well marked, but roughly parallels the creek on the way up and provides a view of a smaller waterfall on the way.

About 20 to 25 minutes from the start you reach a chain-link fence and gate with a British Pacific Properties sign. Go through the gate and continue uphill, still being wary of the steep drop-offs into the canyon, to the dramatic upper falls viewpoint about 5 minutes later. Then follow the trail up some large stone steps before it levels out and widens. About 5 minutes from the upper falls viewpoint you emerge onto a gravelled fire access road. Turn right here and follow this road east and uphill for a couple of minutes to its junction with Eagle Lake Road.

The McCrady Bridge over Cypress Creek is on your right, but follow Eagle Lake Road left and uphill. About 10 minutes later you reach a "Trail Crossing Ahead" sign on your right. Turn left into the woods here on what becomes an overgrown old road, which you follow uphill and west for another 10 minutes to a TCT sign-posted junction. A right turn here would take you toward Cypress Bowl Road, but you go left, following the TCT west. Stay to the left at the next three "Watershed" sign junctions, following the TCT as it curves downhill and into the woods.

In another few minutes, and roughly an hour from the start, you cross the Eagle Creek footbridge, then continue through the forest of large, second-growth trees as the winding path makes its way roughly west and gradually downhill. Although the trail is not well marked, it is fairly easy to follow and there are occasional TCT signs on the trees.

About 25 minutes from Eagle Creek, you reach another TCT signposted junction. Going left here would take you southeast back along the fire access road to the point where you emerged from Cypress Falls Park in a half hour or so, but turn right and down-hill into Nelson Canyon Park. Walk down some stairs and follow this pleasant trail south along the east side of Nelson Creek, which was named after August Nelson, a local framer and planerman who had a mill site at Eagle Harbour in the 1890s. Just beyond the stairs you pass a signposted junction with a connector trail heading west across Nelson Creek toward Whyte Lake (see hike #3) and the Baden-Powell Trail (see hike #17), but you continue south down the TCT.

As the TCT emerges into a clearing a few minutes later, it goes to the right and west, but you stay left, following the winding gravel road downhill. At the next signposted junction, continue straight ahead to go under the highway (not to the right over a 1950s-era bridge). You then go past a yellow gate and out into a small parking area. If you earlier left a car here, turn left onto Westport Road and follow it back to Woodgreen Drive and Woodgreen Place. Otherwise, the walk back is about half an hour.

The footbridge over Eagle Creek.

# 5 ▶ Eagle Bluff and Black Mountain

**Elevation gain:** 310 metres (1,015 feet)
**High point:** 1,224 metres (4,015 feet)
**Season:** July to October
**Topographical map:** North Vancouver 92G06
**Hiking time:** 4 to 5 hours, including lunch
Dog-friendly

Spectacular, breathtaking vistas and a myriad of lovely little subalpine lakes await those who can manage the initial trek up the side of Black Mountain. The hike takes you from the Cypress Mountain ski area up to Eagle Bluff and both Black Mountain summits, passing numerous lakes along the way. It is best done in midsummer to early fall, long after the snow melts and before the fall rains start, as higher-level sections of the trail can be muddy and slippery in places.

From Highway 1 in West Vancouver, you reach the trailhead by taking Exit 8 for Cypress Park, and following Cypress Bowl Road all the way up to the alpine ski area parking lot.

Begin by following the "Baden-Powell Trail (Black Mountain)" arrows from the trailhead signposts north of the parking lot and just past Cypress Creek Lodge. The new, well-marked approach trail leads roughly northwest from the lodge, around the base of the Eagle Express Chair and then west up the side of the ski area. You have a fairly steep, switchbacking uphill slog on this trail before coming out into the subalpine open area in 35 to 45 minutes. The very pretty Cabin Lake, a popular but cold swimming spot during the summer, is just a couple of minutes ahead along the boardwalk.

From the signposted Cabin Lake junction follow the Baden-Powell (BP) dirt trail south into the woods. In about 5 minutes you reach the south summit of Black Mountain at 1,217 metres (3,993 feet), a large rock outcropping on your left with a 360-degree panoramic view, including northeast to Mount Strachan (see hike #7). Continuing south on your way to Eagle Bluff, you next pass Owen Lake then the Cougar Lakes, both on your left. The trail through this area can be muddy in places, although several long boardwalks are a great help, before you descend into the woods on the last stretch to Eagle Bluff.

You will know when you have reached 1,094-metre (3,590-foot) Eagle Bluff, about 2 kilometres (1¼ miles) and 45 minutes from Black Mountain. This viewpoint is absolutely spectacular, with magnificent views across the entire Lower Mainland, as well

Looking southwest from the top of Eagle Bluff, with Bowen Island on the right.

as east to Mount Baker and south to Point Roberts. Looking down and west you see Eagle Lake, Eagle Harbour, Horseshoe Bay, over to Bowen Island and up the Sunshine Coast. This is a good spot for lunch, but be sure to protect your meal from the quite bold whisky jacks and ravens. Looking straight down from Eagle Bluff you get a feeling for the steep descent of the BP Trail as it continues south and then west toward either the newer Nelson Canyon/Whyte Creek trailhead or the original Black Mountain trailhead near the Eagleridge Exit 2 from Highway 1 (see hike #17).

Retracing your steps back uphill and into the woods, you come to a signposted junction about 30 minutes from Eagle Bluff and just past Owen Lake. Go right here, following a short loop trail that takes you past Theagill Lake on your left and Sam Lake on your right. At the next signposted junction, go left to return to the Cabin Lake Trail. In another few minutes you reach the next junction, where you can go right and downhill to the parking lot or left and back to the Cabin Lake junction in a couple of minutes.

From the Cabin Lake junction you can take one more side trip of about 250 metres (820 feet) north to the 1,224-metre (4,015-foot) north summit of Black Mountain (a.k.a. Yew Lake Lookout).

Here you are treated to views of the Lions, the Sea to Sky Highway and as far north as the Tantalus Range. Returning to the Cabin Lake junction, go left and head back downhill to the parking lot, watching your footing on the steep, switchbacking trail.

Black Mountain is also a popular winter hiking destination. A backcountry access pass is required, and available for free at Cypress Creek Lodge. The winter route trail access is the same as the summertime one. You will also need ski poles and either snowshoes or hiking boots with crampons. The trail has frequent marker poles and is easy to follow, although it is fairly steep all the way up. Hiking times are roughly the same as those quoted above for summer hiking.

Hikers arriving at Eagle Bluff from the Black Mountain south summit.

# 6 ▶ St. Mark's Summit

**Elevation gain:** 435 metres (1,425 feet)
**High point:** 1,350 metres (4,430 feet)
**Season:** July to October
**Topographical map:** North Vancouver 92G06
**Hiking time:** 5 to 6 hours, including lunch
Dog-friendly

This hike is a short yet scenic introduction to the 29-kilometre (18-mile) high-level Howe Sound Crest Trail, providing great viewpoints of the Lions to the northeast and magnificent vistas over Howe Sound to the west. The trail continues on to Unnecessary Mountain, the Lions, Deeks Lake and Highway 99 just south of Porteau Cove for those backpackers desiring a much longer and more challenging outing. This hike starts in the Cypress Mountain ski area and takes you 5½ kilometres (3.4 miles) along the Howe Sound Crest Trail to St. Mark's Summit. It is best done in midsummer to early fall, to avoid the snowy and muddy patches that linger well into summer at this elevation.

From Highway 1 in West Vancouver, you reach the trailhead by taking Exit 8 for Cypress Park, and following Cypress Bowl Road 14 kilometres (8.7 miles) up to the alpine ski area parking lot.

Begin by following the directions for the Howe Sound Crest Trail from the trailhead signposts north of the parking lot and just past Cypress Creek Lodge. About 5 minutes later you reach a signposted junction where the Howe Sound Crest Trail West and the Yew Lake Trail are to your left, but you go right for the Howe Sound Crest Trail East (Yew Lake is a "no dogs" area). There is a short ascent into the forest on this first section before you come out, staying left on a wide, gravel road (Pumphouse Road) next to a Mount Strachan ski run. After a few minutes, you go right at a signposted junction just before a large, green water tower, following the somewhat rocky, rooty dirt trail as it switchbacks up into the woods before reaching another gravel road about 10 minutes later.

Going left and continuing along briefly to the end of the road, you head into the woods again, with Black Mountain (see hike #5) visible on your left. This very pleasant trail along the lower western slopes of Mount Strachan is easy to follow and well marked with large, orange metal markers on the trees. About 30 minutes from the start you reach the Binkert Kiosk (named for noted trail builder

Highway 99, Horseshoe Bay and Bowen Island from St. Mark's Summit.

Paul Binkert) and a signposted junction with a 500-metre (1,650-foot) side trail on your left to the Bowen Lookout. This excellent lookout is relatively new, and well worth a look. (Should you decide not to continue on to St. Mark's Summit, it even provides a fine, half-hour loop back to the start via the Howe Sound Crest Trail West.)

A few metres farther along the main trail a viewpoint to the Lions is on your right. About 15 minutes later you emerge from the forest at Strachan Meadows and cross Montizambert Creek. Notice the twin peaks of Mount Strachan up to your right (see hike #7). This is roughly the halfway point in the hike (in distance, not time), and a good spot for a break before tackling another 275 metres (900 feet) of elevation gain.

Back in the forest again, the trail now steepens somewhat as you climb a ridge, following a series of rocky, rooty switchbacks, which could be quite slippery when wet. The trail is still easy to follow, and for the most part you are sheltered from the sun by forest cover. Eventually, after a second similar ridge, the trail levels out and you reach the subalpine meadows of St. Mark's Summit, about an hour and a quarter from Montizambert Creek and roughly two hours from the start.

There are two spectacular viewpoints west over Howe Sound from the rocky knolls, one on each side of the little pond next to the trail. Be wary of going too close to the cliff edge at both of these viewpoints, as it is a very long way down. Looking out to the west you see Horseshoe Bay, Bowen Island, Bowyer Island, Gambier Island and the Sunshine Coast laid out before you. From the more northerly viewpoint you also look directly down at the vehicles on Highway 99.

Off to the north are views of Unnecessary Mountain and the Lions, possible objectives for a very long day's hike another time. For today, after taking in the superb views and enjoying your lunch, retrace your steps back to the parking lot.

Looking over to the Sunshine Coast from St. Mark's Summit.

# 7 ► Mount Strachan

> **Elevation gain:** 525 metres (1,720 feet)
> **High point (south peak):** 1,445 metres (4,740 feet)
> **Season:** July to October
> **Topographical map:** North Vancouver 92G06
> **Hiking time:** 5 to 6½ hours, including lunch
> Dog-friendly

There are several possible approaches to the panoramic viewpoints of the two Mount Strachan summits. This one, along the western slopes of Mount Hollyburn, takes you from the Cypress Mountain ski area east along the Baden-Powell (BP) Trail through some lovely forest groves to meet up with the Old Strachan Trail, a route first used by hikers and mountaineers more than 100 years ago. You follow this trail up to a pass between Hollyburn Peak and Mount Strachan, then through pretty subalpine meadows to Mount Strachan's south summit.

From Highway 1 in West Vancouver, you reach the trailhead by taking Exit 8 for Cypress Park, and following Cypress Bowl Road 14 kilometres (8.7 miles) all the way up to the alpine ski area parking lot.

The Cypress Provincial Park trailhead signposts are located north of the parking lot and just past Cypress Creek Lodge. As a shortcut for this hike, begin by taking the "Baden Powell Trail

(Hollyburn Mountain)" direction on the signpost just behind the First Aid building. You go east and uphill on the ski run for a couple of minutes to where another signpost leads you into the woods. You now gradually gain elevation on an easy-to-follow, undulating forest path through large, second-growth fir and cedar. In 10 to 12 minutes you cross the first of two small Cypress Creek tributaries, then the second one, with a much larger, rockier canyon, less than 5 minutes later.

Immediately after the second creek crossing you go up a short slope then leave the BP by turning left at some orange metal flashings and a wooden "Baden Powell" sign on a tree. Crossing a fallen log, you follow the trail uphill, with the creek on your left. This trail, mostly dirt with lots of roots, has a few wet spots as it climbs steadily. A convenient shortcut to the Old Strachan Trail, it is not well marked, but is quite well worn and fairly easy to follow.

Less than 20 minutes from the BP you reach a junction (marked as 1,055 metres, or 3,460 feet, elevation) with the Old Strachan Trail coming up on your right. This trail continues gradually uphill, with frequent markings on the trees. In 10 to 15 minutes the forest opens up a little to a meadows area, with a small tarn in the trees to your right.

In another few minutes you reach a point in the pass, marked by several large fallen logs, where a very steep trail on your right leads up to Hollyburn Peak (see hike #8). However, you go left here to continue your ascent of Mount Strachan. After another short uphill section you enter a meadows area, with a ski run on your left. In another few minutes you descend a small rock face and pass through another open meadow. Next you commence a fairly steady climb up a rocky, rooty trail, with the ski run still over on your left.

About 15 or 20 minutes from the rock face you reach the site of some wreckage from the tragic 1963 crash of a Royal Canadian Navy T-33 jet trainer, where both Victoria-area crew members were killed. Continuing north and uphill, you climb fairly steeply for about 20 minutes before emerging into subalpine meadows. The Sky Chair is on your left, as are views over to Black Mountain (see hike #5), Vancouver and beyond. In another few minutes, and roughly two hours from the start, you reach Mount Strachan's south peak, with spectacular views in all directions, including Horseshoe Bay, Bowen Island, the Sunshine Coast, the Lions, Coliseum, Crown and Grouse mountains.

The summit is spacious enough to provide many suitable places for a lunch break while you take in the views. You could also descend northwards to the col between the two peaks then climb up to the slightly higher (by 14 metres, or 46 feet) north peak, with its unobstructed views, if time and weather conditions permit. Allow 45 minutes to an hour for the round trip.

When you are ready to return, you can simply retrace your steps back down. If time is an issue, the quickest option is to follow

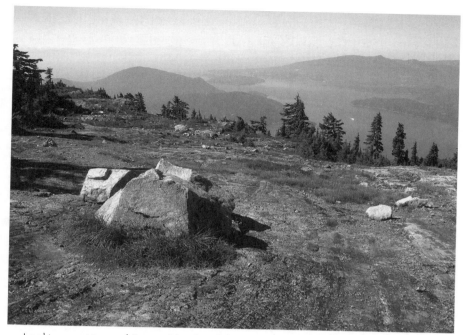

Looking west toward Bowen Island and the Sunshine Coast from Mount Strachan's south peak.

the nearby ski runs all the way back to the parking lot, taking about an hour.

Otherwise, upon reaching the junction of the Old Strachan Trail with your approach trail from the BP (at the 1,055-metre mark) you have two choices: stay right to take the same shortcut, or if time permits, go left to enjoy a longer trek through some magnificent old-growth trees, including an impressive yellow cedar thought to be more than 1,000 years old. Watch for this "Hollyburn Giant," with a height of 20.7 metres (68 feet) to its broken top and a diameter of 3.2 metres (10½ feet), the largest ever recorded in BC, on your right, just a couple of minutes past the trail junction. Continuing down the Old Strachan Trail, you reach its signposted junction with the BP near another Cypress Creek crossing, about half an hour from the Hollyburn Giant.

Here you turn sharp right to stay on the west side of the creek, and follow the BP back to the alpine ski area parking lot in 35 to 45 minutes. Driving back down Cypress Bowl Road, watch for another massive, old-growth yellow cedar on your right, just past the turnoff for the Nordic ski area. A nearby storyboard describes this 1,200-year-old "Roadside Yellow Cedar" as Cypress Park's largest known tree by volume.

Looking north toward the Lions and as far as Mount Garibaldi, from Mount Strachan's north peak.

# 8 ▶ Hollyburn Peak

> **Elevation gain:** 435 metres (1,425 feet)
> **High point:** 1,325 metres (4,350 feet)
> **Season:** July to October
> **Topographical map:** North Vancouver 92G06
> **Hiking time:** 3 to 4 hours
> Dog-friendly

Hollyburn Peak was first climbed in 1908 and is a most rewarding objective with its panoramic mountain views. Today climbing Hollyburn need only be a relatively short, half-day outing, a far cry from the 1920s when hikers would make the trek up old logging trails from the West Vancouver ferry terminus at Ambleside. The hike takes you from the Cypress Mountain Nordic (cross-country) ski area along part of the Baden-Powell (BP) Trail, then up the Hollyburn Mountain Trail to Hollyburn Peak. A short side trip on the way back can take you past First Lake and historic Hollyburn Lodge. This hike is best done in midsummer or early fall, long after the snow melts and before the fall rains start, as the Hollyburn Mountain Trail can be muddy and slippery in places.

From Highway 1 in West Vancouver, you reach the trailhead by taking Exit 8 for Cypress Park, and following Cypress Bowl Road about 13 kilometres (8 miles) up to the Nordic ski area parking lot.

Begin by taking the gravel path uphill from the trailhead kiosk, and going to your left near the woods to follow Powerline Road north. (Going to your right along the power lines would take you to Hollyburn Lodge and First Lake—see hike #10—or take the optional side trip on your return as described below.) Looking over to your left on the way up the trail, you see Black Mountain with its sculptured freestyle skiing and snowboard runs from the 2010 Olympics.

Powerline Road rises fairly steeply for the first few minutes

Hikers on top of Hollyburn Peak.

then crosses under the power lines just before coming to Third Lake, the small lake on your left about 10 to 15 minutes from the start. A couple of minutes later you reach a signposted junction, with a large, green warming hut on your left. Here you turn left as you join the BP coming in from the other side of the power lines. Just past the warming hut is Fourth Lake on your left as the BP heads north into the woods.

The trail, which alternates in and out of forest cover as you go up, is a little rough and rocky in places but easy to follow, even without the orange metal markers on the trees. Blueberries are in abundance on Hollyburn in late summer and it's common to see people picking near the trail, but be aware that bears are often seen eating here as well.

About 40 to 50 minutes and 2.2 kilometres (1.4 miles) from the start you reach the signposted junction where the BP turns off to the west toward Cypress Bowl, but you continue straight ahead and a little more steeply uphill for another 1.9 kilometres (1.2 miles) toward Hollyburn Peak.

About 20 minutes or so from the BP junction a short side

trail to your right leads to a bench and lookout point east toward Crown, Goat and Grouse mountains. A few minutes later you reach a very pretty open area, the Heather Lakes, with its rocky outcroppings and picturesque little ponds.

Another 10 to 15 minutes, with a little scramble up a rocky section at the end, finds you at Hollyburn Peak, with its spectacular vistas in all directions. Landmarks include the twin peaks of Mount Strachan to the northwest (see hike #7) and the Lions to the north, with the snow-capped peaks of the Coast Range beyond. Crown, Grouse and Goat mountains are off to the east, with Cathedral Mountain looming beyond.

There are lots of spots for a lunch or snack break other than the rocky peak itself, but be sure to guard your food from the quite aggressive whisky jacks and ravens. After a well-deserved break, retrace your steps back down to the warming hut at the power lines.

From here you could continue downhill and back to the parking lot. Otherwise, if you have an extra half hour or so, follow the BP straight across the clearing under the power lines and into the woods. Here you begin heading downhill on Upper Wells Gray, one of the major cross-country ski trails. In about 15 minutes you reach a signposted turnoff on your right for a short connector trail to Hollyburn Lodge, originally opened as Hollyburn Ski Camp in early 1927, and very pretty First Lake, the site of an impressive ski jump in those early days. When you have explored enough here, follow the signs from behind the lodge back west to the parking lot in about 10 minutes.

Hollyburn Peak is also a popular winter hiking destination. Starting from the trailhead kiosk, look for the "Backcountry Access" signs near the roadway, as the winter route is not the same as the summertime one. You will need ski poles and either snowshoes or hiking boots with crampons. The trail has marker poles every few metres and is easy to follow (although it gets a little steep and can be quite slippery, depending on snow conditions, near the top).

# 9 ▸ Hollyburn Cabin Country

**Elevation gain:** 190 metres (620 feet)
**High point:** 950 metres (3,115 feet)
**Season:** July to October
**Topographical map:** North Vancouver 92G06
**Hiking time:** 2½ to 3 hours
Dog-friendly

Since the 1920s, generations of Hollyburn hikers and skiers have developed an intricate network of trails and built cabins of every description as bases for their weekend getaways and wilderness adventures. This rewarding trek introduces you to part of that Hollyburn Ridge trail system and some of the eclectic old cabins that remain. The hike takes you on a loop up the old West Lake Road, along part of the Baden-Powell (BP) Trail to First Lake and Hollyburn Lodge, then down the old Forks Trail back to the start. It is best done in midsummer to early fall, after the snow melts and before the fall rains start, as higher-level sections of these trails can be muddy and slippery in places.

From Highway 1 in West Vancouver you reach the trailhead by taking Exit 8 for Cypress Park and following Cypress Bowl Road up for about 11 kilometres (7 miles), passing first Highview Lookout and then Quarry Lookout. Just past the next hairpin turn there is a gravel parking area on the right-hand side for access to West Lake Road.

Begin by following this wide, gravel service road uphill, staying right at two junctions with other gravel roads. In 10 minutes or so you pass a yellow gate blocking further vehicle access to the area, then cross a bridge over Marr Creek. Stay right at the next trail junction, and about 10 minutes past Marr Creek you reach a signposted junction with a small trail on your right. This trail, actually the most northerly piece of the Old Brewis Trail (see hike #12), leads gradually downhill and is fairly easy to follow, with occasional red markers on the trees. In just a few minutes you come to a decrepit old log cabin, minus its roof, about 20 metres (65 feet) over to your left. It looks old enough to be one of the originals from the early 1900s. Just ahead the trail descends to a steep and challenging crossing of the east branch of McDonald Creek, so retrace your steps back uphill to the West Lake Road trail.

Continue uphill on this rough, rocky road, staying left at the next two forks in the road. About 15 minutes from the Brewis

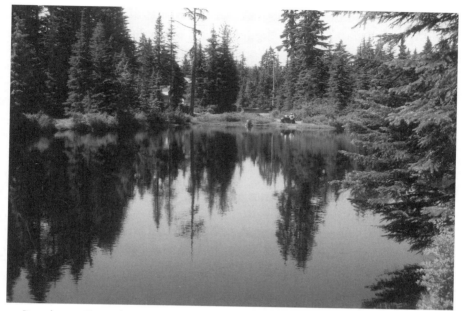

Picnickers at First Lake, with Hollyburn Lodge to the left.

Trail side trip you reach a large, open area, the site of the former Westlake Ski Lodge, which was originally moved piecemeal from West Lake in 1938 but which burned to the ground over 20 years ago. Go left at the BP Trail signpost just ahead and continue uphill toward the cross-country ski area, saving the access trail to Blue Gentian Lake, a few metres ahead on your right, for another day (see hike #10).

Turn right at the next BP signpost a couple of minutes later to go up a narrow, rocky trail with views east to Indian Arm and Mount Baker on a good day. Go right at the next BP signposted junction, where the BP becomes a wide, cross-country ski trail (the Grand National). As you continue up, stay left on the Grand National at the Jack Pratt junction. Next you pass an access trail on your right for West Lake (again a good outing for another day; see hike #10), followed by a couple of private cabins.

At the next signposted junction, 20 to 25 minutes from the Westlake Ski Lodge site, the BP continues north, but you follow the sign left for the Burfield Trail to reach First Lake. Once you've had a look around First Lake and Hollyburn Lodge (which was operated by the Burfield family from 1946 to 1984), return to the Nasmyth Bridge over Marr Creek at the south end of the lake and locate the sign for the Forks Trail, next to a large trail map.

Follow the Forks Trail downhill, with Marr Creek on your left, noting the numerous private cabins secluded in the woods on either side. About 10 minutes later, stay left at the "Trail" sign junction, following this very pleasant, winding trail gradually downhill through more cabin country. About 15 to 20 minutes from the start, the trail becomes a fine gravel path. One branch leads left to more cabins on the other side of a well-built footbridge over Marr Creek and the other continues downhill.

Staying to the right and continuing downhill, you reach a large gravel parking area a couple of minutes later. Go right here and follow the gravel road downhill. About 5 minutes later you reach its junction with West Lake Road, where you go right again and retrace your steps back out to Cypress Bowl Road and your car.

Otherwise, going left and crossing the bridge provides an alternate return route. There is an old picnic table and bench on your right a couple of minutes across the bridge. In the brush nearby are concrete footings from the terminus of the old Hollyburn chairlift, built in 1950 but destroyed in a fire in 1965. This is also the site of the former Hi-View Lodge, built in the early 1950s but burned down in the same fire.

At the four-way trail junction another couple of minutes on, there are three options. If you have time for some more exploring, the gravel road on your left takes you past a few cabins and back up to First Lake in 15 to 20 minutes. Continuing on the trail straight ahead takes you past some more cabins and back to the Westlake Ski Lodge site in the same amount of time. Otherwise, go down to your right to reach West Lake Road in less than 5 minutes. Turn right here and retrace your steps back across Marr Creek, past the yellow gate and out to Cypress Bowl Road in about 10 minutes.

# 10 ► Hollyburn Lakes Circuit

**Elevation gain:** 220 metres (720 feet)
**High point:** 950 metres (3,115 feet)
**Season:** July to October
**Topographical map:** North Vancouver 92G06
**Hiking time:** 3 to 3½ hours
Dog-friendly

Hollyburn Ridge is blessed with numerous pretty little subalpine lakes to attract the hiker. This rewarding circuit of its trail system treats you to four of these lakes in one outing, with only moderate elevation gain along the way. You go through the Cypress Mountain Nordic (cross-country) ski area to Hollyburn Lodge and First Lake, then around to West Lake, Lost Lake and Blue Gentian Lake before heading back. This hike is best done in midsummer to early fall, long after the snow melts and before the fall rains start, as some of these trails can be muddy and slippery in places.

From Highway 1 in West Vancouver, you reach the trailhead by taking Exit 8 for Cypress Park, and following Cypress Bowl Road about 13 kilometres (8 miles) up to the Nordic ski area parking lot.

Begin by following the gravel path uphill from the trailhead kiosk, staying to your right near the woods (going left along the power lines leads up toward Hollyburn Peak; see hike #8) and taking the ski trail east under the "Hollyburn Trail to Hollyburn

Lodge" sign. In about 10 minutes you pass a quaint, 1930s-era rental cabin on your left. Next you reach the red Hollyburn Lodge, originally opened as Hollyburn Ski Camp in early 1927, and First Lake, the site of an impressive ski jump in those early days. Go past the ranger station, crossing the Nasmyth Bridge over Marr Creek at the south end of the lake, and up the dirt road to the sign-posted Baden-Powell (BP) Trail junction. Turn right and follow the BP downhill for about 5 minutes to the West Lake Trail signpost.

Go left here to follow this wide, dirt trail for about 10 minutes to West Lake. This spot was the site of the original West Lake Lodge, which was opened in 1933 but closed and dismantled in 1938 when West Vancouver wanted to include the area in the Brothers Creek watershed. Part of the structure of a ski jump built in 1934 can still be seen in the water at the north end of the lake.

From West Lake, take the signposted 440-metre (1,440-foot) trail for Blue Gentian Lake, following Stoney Creek south and downhill. The trail is quite easy to follow, but is fairly rough and can be muddy in places. At the next signposted junction, go left for the Lost Lake/Blue Gentian Lake Trail. In another few minutes you see Blue Gentian Lake on your right, but save that detour for

West Lake, near the site of the original 1930s West Lake Lodge.

the way back and take the Lost Lake Trail to the left. This trail is rougher and not as well marked as the others. It crosses first Stoney Creek and then Brothers Creek (without footbridges, so take care if water levels are high), taking you to Lost Lake (originally known as East Lake) in another 25 to 35 minutes.

Leaving Lost Lake, take the trail on the right-hand side, heading south and downhill. In about 400 metres (1,315 feet) and another 10 to 15 minutes you come to Brothers Creek again. The trail down to your left is the fire access road heading south, but you take the footbridge across the creek then go to your right, up the Brothers Creek Trail toward Blue Gentian Lake. This pleasant trail has markers on the trees and is quite easy to follow. In 20 to 30 minutes you reach Blue Gentian Lake (known as Middle Lake back in the 1920s), where you can rest at the lakeside picnic table.

Next, follow the boardwalk around to the west side of the lake, passing the trail junction for the other lakes on your right. If you are there in late summer, watch for the lake's namesake king gentian flowers near the boardwalk before heading into the woods on the 300-metre (985-foot) trail to the BP junction.

Go right here to follow the BP uphill. In about 5 minutes you come to a large clearing, the second site of the West Lake Lodge, which was moved piecemeal from West Lake and reconstructed here in 1938 as the Westlake Ski Lodge. It was later renamed Cypress Park Resort, but after almost 50 years of operation it burned to the ground in 1986.

Go right at the signposted junction to continue uphill on the wide, rocky BP. At the next clearing, in about 5 more minutes, follow the BP to the right into the woods and up a narrow, rocky trail with views east to Indian Arm and Mount Baker. At the next signposted junction, in another 5 minutes, go right as the BP becomes the Grand National ski trail. As you continue up, stay left on the Grand National at the Jack Pratt junction. On your way up you pass the turnoff you took earlier for West Lake.

About 20 to 25 minutes from the West Lake Lodge site you reach another signposted junction. Here the BP continues north, but you follow the sign left for the Burfield Trail, retracing your steps to First Lake, Hollyburn Lodge and then the parking lot.

A 1930s-era rental cabin near Hollyburn Lodge.

# 11 ▶ Trans Canada Trail/ Millstream Trail Loop

> **Elevation gain:** 290 metres (950 feet)
> **High point:** 670 metres (2,200 feet)
> **Season:** May to November
> **Topographical map:** North Vancouver 92G06
> **Hiking time:** 2½ to 3 hours
> Dog-friendly

This ambitious but rewarding trek on the slopes of lower Hollyburn treats you to a variety of terrain and crossings of several major West Vancouver creeks. It also passes Highview Lookout on Cypress Bowl Road and includes a visit to the Shields Log Dam and Flume Pond from the early 1900s. The hike follows part of the Lawson Creek Forestry Heritage Walk (named for John Lawson, one of West Vancouver's leading pioneers, and responsible for several major community achievements during the early 1900s), as it takes you from the lower Millstream Road trailhead, up the Brewis Trail, then west along the Trans Canada Trail (TCT) to the Forks Trail for a loop back along the Millstream Trail.

From Highway 1 in West Vancouver you reach the trailhead by taking Exit 11, going north on Crosscreek Road, then left onto Chartwell Drive, following Chartwell up to its intersection with

Eyremount Drive and Millstream Road, where there is a yellow gate marking the trailhead.

Begin by going west from the gate along the dirt road for about 10 minutes, passing a signposted junction with a fire access road and then crossing Lawson Creek before coming to the Brewis Trail junction on your right. This trail is not well marked, but easy to follow. You climb steadily uphill for 20 to 30 minutes before coming to the TCT/Skyline Trail at the power lines, where you go left.

Watch for the occasional yellow TCT sign on the trees, and follow this very pleasant trail west as it moves alternately from forest cover to open stretches under the power lines. It crosses several creeks along the way, with deep ravines for the three different branches of McDonald Creek and then Marr Creek. After 40 to 50 minutes from the Brewis Trail junction, you reach the TCT/Skyline Trail's junction with the Forks Trail, marked by a TCT signpost.

The TCT/Skyline Trail continues west, while the branch of the Forks Trail a few metres ahead on your right heads north, leading up toward West Lake Road, Hollyburn cabin country and Hollyburn Lodge (see hike #9). You go down to the left, following the Forks Trail in a generally southeasterly direction. It is rough and not well marked, but fairly well worn and easy to follow.

Outlet of the 1920s' Shields Log Dam and Flume Pond.

This trail is steep in places and also used by mountain bikers, so be alert for bikers coming down quickly behind you. After 25 to 30 minutes of downhill travel, you cross Marr Creek again, and in about another 5 minutes you come to an unmarked (other than by a large "British Pacific Properties" sign on a tree) junction with the Millstream Trail heading east.

You can see Highview Lookout (a.k.a. Barrett's View since 2012, named after former BC Premier Dave Barrett) on Cypress Bowl Road through the trees, and may want to take a slight detour to the right to check out this spectacular view. Otherwise, take the Millstream Trail to your left (east), bearing slightly uphill before descending to the first footbridge. In 10 to 15 minutes, after crossing all three branches of McDonald Creek again, the trail widens out to look more like the old logging road that it is. Continue following it east for 25 to 30 minutes from the lookout to a chain-link fence and gate next to a signposted junction with a trail leading down to Pinecrest Drive.

Before returning to Millstream Road, if time permits, go down this winding trail for a couple of minutes to the Shields Dam Park, the site of the Shields Log Dam and Flume Pond. Built in 1917 and used until 1926, the dam and pond were designed to store floating cedar shingle bolts (long, wedge-shaped blocks of cedar from which shakes and shingles were cut) and to supply water to the wooden flume that transported the shingle bolts to the Vedder shingle mill. The mill was once located on Lawson Creek at Inglewood Avenue and 18th Street (now Sinclair), roughly 2 kilometres (1¼ miles) below. In its nine years of operation the mill employed up to 90 men and had the capacity to produce 360,000 shingles per day.

To return to your car, go back up to the Millstream Trail junction, turn right, cross the Lawson Creek footbridge and retrace your steps out to the Millstream Road gate.

A double footbridge over Lawson Creek on the Millstream Trail.

# 12 ▶ The Old Brewis Trail

| |
|---|
| **Elevation gain:** 280 metres (920 feet)<br>**High point:** 660 metres (2,165 feet)<br>**Season:** May to November<br>**Topographical map:** North Vancouver 92G06<br>**Hiking time:** 2 to 2½ hours<br>Dog-friendly |

Here is another energetic outing that closely follows the Lawson Creek Forestry Heritage Walk and passes historical remnants of early 1900s' logging activities as well as the massive, 1,100-year-old Hollyburn Fir. The hike takes you from the lower Millstream Road trailhead, partway up Brothers Creek, then along the Crossover Trail to the Old Brewis Trail for a loop back to the start. The Brewis name has long been associated with the Hollyburn area; R.D. Brewis built the original West Lake Lodge in the winter of 1932–33.

From Highway 1 in West Vancouver, you reach the trailhead by taking Exit 11, going north on Crosscreek Road, then left onto Chartwell Drive, following Chartwell up to its intersection with Eyremount Drive and Millstream Road, where there is a yellow gate marking the trailhead.

Begin by going west along the dirt road for about 5 minutes until you reach a signposted junction with the fire access road leading north. Turn right and follow this road uphill, passing through a chain-link gate before you come to a signposted junction for the Shields Incline Railway. The railway was part of an old cable system built in the early 1920s to transport cedar shingle bolts (long, wedge-shaped blocks of cedar from which shakes and shingles were cut) down the mountainside to the Shields Log Dam and Flume Pond. It was abandoned in 1926. Turn right and follow

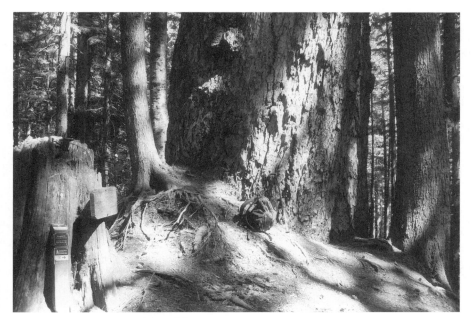

The giant 1,100-year-old Hollyburn Fir.

this trail uphill for about 10 minutes until you come to a signpost for Brothers Creek.

Go left here up the west side of Brothers Creek for another few minutes until you come to a signpost directing you to the right. Continue uphill, noting a large granite rock on your right, a glacial erratic from the last ice age about 12,000 years ago. In another few minutes you come to a signposted junction with the Baden-Powell/Trans Canada Trail (BP/TCT) at the power lines. Turn left, following the BP/TCT past an old BC Hydro helicopter pad on your right. In about 5 minutes you come to a signposted junction where the BP/TCT continues west, but you turn right to follow the Brothers Creek trail north.

Continue steadily uphill alongside Brothers Creek, being wary of some steep drop-offs into the canyon on your right. In 10 to 15 minutes you pass a signposted junction with the Crossover Trail on your right. Continue straight ahead about 25 more metres (80 feet), then go left on the Crossover Trail, heading west toward the Old Brewis Trail. The trail crosses several old skid roads and is difficult to follow in places, but there are occasional red metal markers on the trees. You cross the BP again in 15 to 20 minutes and then Lawson Creek a few metres farther on.

After another 10 minutes or so you reach the signposted site of the giant Hollyburn Fir on your right. This living Douglas fir, rising 45 metres (150 feet) to its broken top, is about 3 metres (10 feet) in diameter and thought to be almost 1,100 years old. The tree was spared during the early 1900s because loggers were mainly interested in the western red cedar. It was rediscovered in 1985 during the Big Tree Registry project of the Ministry of Forests.

Just past the Hollyburn Fir you reach the Crossover Trail's junction with the Old Brewis Trail. To the right the Brewis leads up to a steep and challenging crossing of McDonald Creek's east branch, then beyond that to West Lake Road, from which you can reach Hollyburn cabin country and Hollyburn Lodge (see hike #9). But you go left, following the red markers on the trees to take the Brewis downhill for about 15 minutes to the TCT/Skyline Trail at the power lines.

Go left along this trail for about 150 metres (500 feet) until you reach the signposted junction with the Lower Brewis Trail. This trail is not well marked, but easy to follow. After 15 minutes or so of downhill you reach the Millstream Trail junction. Turn left here, following the trail east for a couple of minutes to a chain-link fence and gate next to a signposted junction with a trail leading down to Pinecrest Drive.

Before returning to Millstream Road, if time permits, go down this winding trail for a couple of minutes to the Shields Dam Park. This is the site of the Shields Log Dam and Flume Pond, built in 1917 and used until 1926 to store floating cedar shingle bolts, and to supply water to the wooden flume that transported the shingle bolts to the bustling Vedder shingle mill 2 kilometres (1¼ miles) below. To return to your car, go back up to the Millstream Trail junction, turn right, cross the Lawson Creek footbridge and retrace your steps out to the Millstream Road gate.

# 13 ► Upper Brothers Creek

**Elevation gain:** 340 metres (1,115 feet)
**High point:** 720 metres (2,360 feet)
**Season:** May to November
**Topographical map:** North Vancouver 92G06
**Hiking time:** 2 to 2½ hours
Dog-friendly

On this hike along part of the Brothers Creek Forestry Heritage Walk, you enjoy breathtaking views of the Brothers Creek upper canyon and waterfalls and pass by some magnificent examples of old-growth cedar and fir on the way back. Starting from the upper Millstream Road trailhead, you go along the Crossover Trail to the upper part of Brothers Creek, then circle back to Millstream via the Brothers Creek fire access road.

From Highway 1 in West Vancouver you reach the trailhead by taking Exit 11, going north on Crosscreek Road, left onto Chartwell Drive, then onto Millstream Road, staying left on Millstream to park just past Henlow Road.

Begin by going through the fire road gate and following the wide, rocky trail (formerly the path of the Walking Dudley, a steam locomotive used by the McNair-Fraser Lumber Company to transport logs down to the West Vancouver waterfront from 1908 to 1913) for about 5 minutes to a signposted junction with the

Baden-Powell/Trans Canada Trail (BP/TCT) at Hadden Creek. Turn left here and then right at the power lines junction to follow the Brothers Creek fire access road into the woods. In another 10 to 15 minutes you reach a signposted junction with the Crossover Trail on your left. Follow this trail west toward Brothers Creek.

In a few minutes you reach a signposted junction with a long, straight trail angled roughly northeast-southwest down the hill. This is the Shields Incline Railway, part of an old cable railway built in the early 1920s to transport cedar shingle bolts (long, wedge-shaped blocks of cedar from which shakes and shingles were cut) down to a shingle mill several kilometres below, but abandoned in 1926. Cross the old railway bed and continue straight ahead up

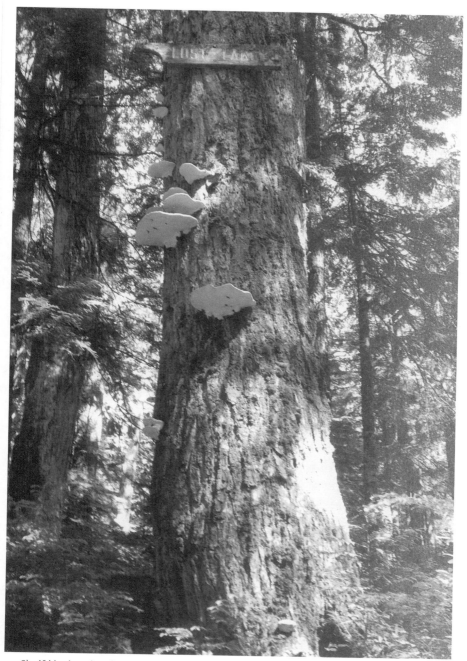

Shelf-like bracket fungi and an old sign pointing the way to Lost Lake decorate a large Douglas fir at the upper Brothers Creek footbridge.

the hill on the Crossover Trail, following the occasional orange markers on the trees.

Soon you begin to hear Brothers Creek on your left and in 15 to 20 minutes from the Incline Railway you reach the footbridge to the other side. Cross the bridge and turn up to your right. In about 25 metres (80 feet) the Crossover Trail continues west toward the BP and Brewis trails (see hike #12), but you stay right, taking the Brothers Creek Trail north. Continue following this very pleasant trail gradually uphill, but be wary of some steep drop-offs into the canyon on your right. Watch for an impressive double waterfall about 20 minutes from the Crossover Trail junction. Some 5 minutes past the waterfall you reach another footbridge across Brothers Creek.

Cross here, leaving the trails to Blue Gentian Lake and Lost Lake (on the east side of the bridge) for another day (see hike #10), and take the wide, rocky fire access road downhill to your right. On the way down watch for some of the magnificent old-growth western red cedar and Douglas fir trees.

About 25 to 30 minutes from the footbridge you come to a switchback where the trail turns sharply to the right. Here you see a small signpost (labelled "#5 & #6") on your left. A short trail with small red markers on the trees leads straight ahead into the forest. In about 7 minutes you reach the pitchfork-like Candelabra tree, a dead, old-growth Douglas fir about 60 metres (200 feet) in height and 3 metres (10 feet) in diameter. Follow the red markers downhill another 3 minutes or so to a tall, living old-growth Douglas fir of a similar diameter.

Retrace your steps back up to the fire access road and continue to follow it downhill. After about 20 minutes, at its junction with the Ballantree–Kildonan Trail (see hike #14) on your left, check out what remains of an old mill boiler house and steam sawmill site, built in 1912 but abandoned in 1913. Then continue downhill, reaching the junction with the BP/TCT trail at the power lines in another few minutes. Go down to your left, where in a couple of minutes you reach the Hadden Creek junction again. Take the trail down to the right and back out to Millstream Road.

# 14 ► Brothers Creek/Ballantree Park

**Elevation gain:** 240 metres (790 feet)
**High point:** 620 metres (2,040 feet)
**Season:** May to November
**Topographical map:** North Vancouver 92G06
**Hiking time:** 2½ to 3½ hours
Dog-friendly

Here is a challenging yet rewarding circuit, with canyon and waterfall views, a lovely trek through a little-known forested West Vancouver park and a visit to relics of early 1900s' logging activity along the way. This hike, which follows part of the Brothers Creek Forestry Heritage Walk, takes you from the lower Millstream Road trailhead, partway up Brothers Creek, over to Ballantree Park via the Crossover Trail, then back to Millstream via the Baden-Powell/ Trans Canada Trail (BP/TCT).

From Highway 1 in West Vancouver you reach the trailhead by taking Exit 11, going north on Crosscreek Road, then left onto Chartwell Drive, following Chartwell up to its intersection with Eyremount Drive and Millstream Road, where there is a yellow gate marking the trailhead.

Begin by going west along the dirt road for about 5 minutes until you reach a signposted junction with the fire access road heading north. Turn right and follow this road uphill, passing a chain-link gate and then a signposted junction for the Shields Incline Railway. This railway was part of an old cable system built in the early 1920s to transport cedar shingle bolts (long, wedge-shaped blocks of cedar from which shakes and shingles were cut) down the mountainside to the Shields Log Dam and Flume Pond, but abandoned in 1926. It will be part of your return route. Continue uphill on the winding dirt road until after 25 to 30 minutes from the start you reach a signposted junction with the BP/TCT. Turn right, following this trail under the power lines and into the woods again, heading east on the BP/TCT. Go left at its signposted junction with the Brothers Creek Trail a few minutes later.

Continue steadily uphill alongside Brothers Creek, being wary of some steep drop-offs into the canyon on your right. After another 10 to 15 minutes you come to a footbridge across Brothers Creek. Cross here and follow the Crossover Trail southeast and downhill. In about 15 minutes, just after a small footbridge, you reach a signposted junction with a long, straight trail angled roughly northeast-southwest down the hill. This is another section

The Brothers Creek lower falls in spring runoff.

of the Incline Railway you passed earlier. Continue downhill on the Crossover Trail for another 5 minutes or so, when you reach its signposted junction with the Brothers Creek fire access road. Turn right to follow this road downhill. In about 10 minutes you reach its signposted junction with the Ballantree–Kildonan trail. Before going left here, check out the remains of the old mill boiler house and steam sawmill site mentioned in hike #13.

The Ballantree–Kildonan trail is a fairly old, easy-to-follow, pleasing trail, albeit with only occasional red markers on the trees. It makes its way uphill in a generally northeasterly direction, then curves gradually southeasterly and downhill. After about a half hour from the fire access road you reach a Ballantree Trail signpost. Go down to the right here, across a footbridge, then to the left and over a second footbridge. Stay to your right through an open area in about 5 minutes, then continue straight ahead and roughly south on the winding dirt path. About 10 minutes from the Ballantree Trail signpost you emerge at the top of Kildonan Road.

Follow Kildonan down to Craigmohr Drive, continuing down to the Millstream Road/Craigmohr intersection a couple of minutes later. On your right is a BP/TCT signpost, where you go up the stairs and follow the trail into the forest, paralleling the power lines on your left-hand side. About 10 minutes later you reach the Hadden Creek signposted junction, where you stay to the right, taking a gravel road back uphill. Stay left at the fire access road junction to follow the BP/TCT west, back under the power lines and into the woods as it gradually gains some elevation.

In about 20 minutes you pass another signposted junction with the Incline Railway. In another few minutes you begin to hear Brothers Creek and you pass a lookout spot with views of Stanley Park, downtown Vancouver and beyond. Descend to a footbridge for the Brothers Creek crossing, with its very impressive waterfall during spring runoff. Just after climbing up from the Brothers Creek canyon, go left and downhill at a BP/TCT signposted junction onto a lower section of the Brothers Creek Trail.

In about 10 minutes you come to its unmarked junction with the Incline Railway, where you turn right to follow this old railway bed southwest and downhill. In another 10 minutes or so you reach its junction with the fire access road. From here you go left and retrace your steps back down to the Millstream Trail then left and out to Millstream Road.

A light dusting of snow along the Millstream Trail.

# 15 ► Ballantree Park from Cleveland Dam

**Elevation gain:** 330 metres (1,080 feet)
**High point:** 480 metres (1,575 feet)
**Season:** April to November
**Topographical map:** North Vancouver 92G06
**Hiking time:** 2 to 2½ hours
Dog-friendly

Here is a hike that truly offers some variety, with stunning views from Cleveland Dam in North Vancouver to the secluded forests of Ballantree Park in West Vancouver. You follow the Baden-Powell (BP) Trail from Cleveland Dam up into West Vancouver, take the Ballantree–Kildonan Trail around Ballantree Park, then return to Cleveland Dam.

You can shorten the hiking time by 40 minutes or so by leaving a second car at the upper Millstream Road trailhead in West Vancouver. That trailhead is reached by taking Exit 11 on Highway 1, going north on Crosscreek Road, left onto Chartwell Drive, then onto Millstream, and staying left on Millstream to park just after passing Henlow Road.

From Highway 1 in North Vancouver take Exit 14 to go north on Capilano Road. Follow it up to the paved parking lot on your left, just past Clements Avenue but before Nancy Greene Way heads up toward Grouse Mountain.

Begin by walking across Cleveland Dam, admiring the views of Capilano Lake, the Lions and Grouse Mountain up on your right, then the awe-inspiring spillway and vertical canyon walls to your left. This dam was completed in 1954 and named after Ernest A. Cleveland, the first chief commissioner of the Greater Vancouver Water District from 1926 to 1952. Across the dam you see two gravel roads on your left. The lower one leads into Capilano Canyon, a good destination for another day (see hike #21), but you take the upper one with the BP signplate.

The BP is well marked with orange "BP" fleur-de-lis triangles on the trees. Follow it uphill, passing two Shinglebolt Trail junctions on your left. About 10 minutes from the dam, just before coming to a chain-link fence at the end of the road, you turn left into the woods at a BP signpost. The trail begins with a fairly steep but short uphill, followed by a brief downhill before emerging onto Glenmore Drive in another 5 minutes or so. Pick up the trail directly across Glenmore Drive, following it west as it begins a gradual ascent through the residential areas of the British Properties. You continue uphill, following the power lines, crossing three more streets and noting the TCT (Trans Canada Trail) and BP markers as you go.

After 25 to 40 minutes of steady climbing on the BP/TCT from

Old mill boiler house and steam sawmill site from 1912–13.

Glenmore Drive, you come to a green metal gate and a Millstream Road/Craigmohr Drive street sign. Turn right here up Craigmohr, then after a couple of minutes go left onto Kildonan Road. In about another 5 minutes you reach the Ballantree Park trailhead at the top of Kildonan.

Follow the trail roughly north into the woods, keeping to the left when you reach an open area in about 5 minutes. In another couple of minutes you see a footbridge over a small creek on your left. Cross the creek, then go right and cross a second footbridge. Next you see the Ballantree Trail signpost, informing you that you will reach the fire access road junction in about 30 minutes, or 1.6 kilometres (1 mile). This is a fairly old, well-worn and easy-to-follow trail, albeit with only occasional red square markers on the trees. In wet weather it can be a bit like a streambed as it makes its way uphill in a generally northwesterly direction, then curves generally southwesterly and downhill. After roughly half an hour you come to the signposted junction with the Brothers Creek fire access road.

Turn left here and check out what remains of an old mill boiler house and steam sawmill site, built in 1912 but abandoned in 1913. Continue downhill, and in 5 minutes you reach the junction with the BP/TCT Trail at the power lines. Go down to your left, where in a couple of minutes you come to another signposted junction at Hadden Creek, about 1¼ to 1¾ hours after leaving Cleveland Dam. If you had earlier left a car at the upper Millstream Road trailhead, you now take the trail down to the right and in 5 minutes you are out on the road.

Otherwise, go to your left, following the BP/TCT/Skyline Trail into the woods as it parallels the power lines east to the Millstream Road/Craigmohr Drive junction. From here you retrace your steps back to Cleveland Dam and the parking lot. The return trip is about 40 minutes from the Hadden Creek junction.

Signpost at the eastern end of the Ballantree Trail.

# 16 ▸ Capilano Pacific Trail

Elevation gain: minimal
High point: 150 metres (490 feet)
Season: Year-round
Topographical map: North Vancouver 92G06
Hiking time: 2 to 2½ hours
Dog-friendly

This all-season trek is a great way to explore some of the lush forest trails of Capilano River Regional Park. Using the upper half of the scenic Capilano Pacific Trail, you start near the eastern end of Keith Road in West Vancouver and through a gradual ascent reach the lovely park setting of Capilano Lake and Cleveland Dam. There are also opportunities for more extensive explorations of Capilano Canyon itself, where this hike intersects with its trails (see hike #21). The Capilano Pacific Trail is the route of the 8½-kilometre (5.3-mile) Coho Walk each September from Cleveland Dam to Ambleside Park in West Vancouver.

From Highway 1 in West Vancouver, take Exit 13 to go south on Taylor Way. Turn left at its intersection with Keith Road, and follow Keith Road east to the parking area, reached just after passing under the Highway 1 bridge across the Capilano River.

You begin by heading north on the Capilano Pacific Trail, which for the first 5 minutes or so is a winding, gravel road, before

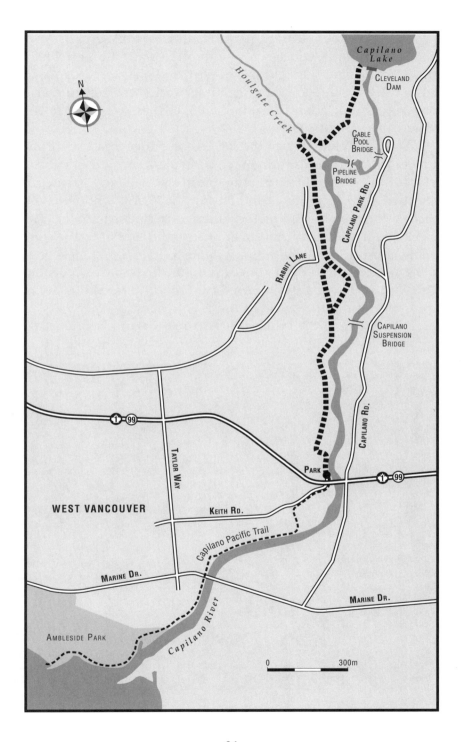

becoming a wide, pleasant path, leading steadily uphill. After about 20 minutes you reach a signposted trail junction where the path down to the right passes next to the enclosed Capilano Suspension Bridge area. Either route works (the left one also provides an exit point to Rabbit Lane), as they reconnect in the woods a few minutes later.

About 10 minutes from the suspension bridge area a short side trail to your right leads to an observation platform with a dramatic view of the canyon. Continuing on up the Capilano Pacific for another 10 to 15 minutes and crossing several footbridges, you reach a long, high, curving footbridge over Houlgate Creek. The creek was named after a member of a syndicate that in the early 1900s constructed a long wooden flume to transport shingle bolts (long wedge-shaped blocks of cedar from which shakes and shingles were cut) from a steam sawmill at Sisters Creek, a tributary of the Capilano, all the way down the river to Burrard Inlet.

After crossing the bridge, follow the Capilano Pacific past a connector to the Shinglebolt Trail coming down from your left. A

The Houlgate Creek footbridge on the Capilano Pacific Trail.

couple of minutes later continue straight ahead to remain on the Capilano Pacific at a signposted junction where the Shinglebolt Trail descends to a Pipeline Bridge crossing of the Capilano River (unless you wish to cross the bridge and spend some extra time exploring Capilano Canyon, using hike #21 for guidance).

Continuing up the Capilano Pacific for another 2 or 3 minutes, you join a wide, gravel road approaching from the lower right. Going sharply right and downhill here for about 50 metres (165 feet) will take you to a signposted trail junction and a second opportunity to explore some of Capilano Canyon's attractions, such as the Giant Fir Trail, Second Canyon Viewpoint, Cable Pool Bridge and fish hatchery (again using hike #21 for guidance).

Otherwise, continue along your gradual ascent of the Capilano Pacific for another few minutes. Roughly an hour or so from the start you emerge from the forested area of Capilano Canyon to reach Cleveland Dam, with its spectacular 90-metre (300-foot) spillway, and views to the north of Capilano Lake, the Lions and Grouse Mountain. Capilano Lake supplies approximately 40 percent of Metro Vancouver's fresh drinking water. Cleveland Dam was completed in 1954 and named after the first chief commissioner of the Greater Vancouver Water District.

Public washrooms, picnic tables and a water fountain are located at the other side of the dam. For your return trip, you can simply retrace your steps back down the Capilano Pacific or choose to explore more of Capilano Canyon itself, using hike #21 for guidance, then rejoining the Capilano Pacific lower down, from the west side of the Pipeline Bridge.

# BADEN-POWELL TRAIL

## Introduction

The Baden-Powell (BP) Trail, named after Boy Scout founder Lord Robert Baden-Powell, was completed in 1971 by Boy Scout and Girl Guide troops to mark BC's 100th birthday. It is a challenging and scenic 48-kilometre (30-mile) route that traverses the North Shore mountains from its western end near Horseshoe Bay in West Vancouver to Deep Cove in North Vancouver. There are some spectacular viewpoints and very pleasant, rewarding sections of trail, but also some especially demanding, strenuous ones.

In theory the entire BP Trail could be covered in one very long day of at least 16 hours, depending on your fitness level and the number of daylight hours available. This option is definitely not advisable, although it is quite possible to tackle the West Vancouver half in one very long day, and the North Vancouver half another day. Fortunately there are many possible access points along the way to break it up into more manageable chunks of several hours each. I have divided the route into four segments, each about 12 kilometres (7½ miles) long. For all but the first one, from the western end to Cypress Bowl, I have also provided an intermediate access/departure point, to shorten the hike if so desired.

The four segments, with time estimates, are:
- Western end to Cypress Bowl (5 to 6½ hours);
- Cypress Bowl to Cleveland Dam (3½ to 4½ hours);
- Grouse Mountain to Lynn Canyon (3¼ to 4 hours);

• Lynn Canyon to Deep Cove (3½ to 4½ hours).

The first segment is by far the most challenging one, with its elevation gain of just over 1,000 metres (3,300 feet), and should only be attempted by experienced hikers in good physical condition. Winter snow conditions on Black Mountain, Cypress and Hollyburn shorten the hiking season for the two West Vancouver segments, while the two North Vancouver ones are good much of the year, depending on the severity of winter season snowfalls.

The annual Knee Knackering North Shore Trail Run, which follows this route almost exactly, has a website, kneeknacker.com, with a detailed course description, course profile and course map under the "Race/Course info" tab. It may be humbling to know that the winners finish the whole course in just under 5 hours, with the laggards finishing in under 10 hours.

Navigating the BP Trail itself is relatively straightforward in most places. The entire trail is well marked with orange "BP" fleur-de-lis triangles on the trees. At major trail junctions there are signposts with distances and estimated completion times. Also, many signposts in the last segment have small trail maps attached.

Since these four are all one-way hikes, car transportation or public transit should be arranged for both ends.

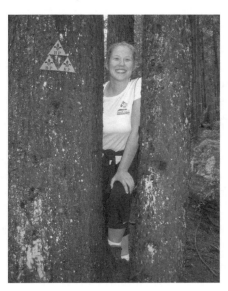

A happy hiker on the Baden-Powell Trail, North Vancouver.

# 17 ▸ Baden-Powell #1, Western End to Cypress Bowl

> **Elevation gain:** 1,087 metres (3,570 feet)
> **High point:** 1,217 metres (3,990 feet)
> **Season:** July to October
> **Topographical map:** North Vancouver 92G06
> **Hiking time:** 5 to 6½ hours, including lunch
> Dog-friendly

Starting from the west, this first 12-kilometre (7½-mile) segment of the Baden-Powell (BP) is by far the most challenging and demanding, with its long slog up to Eagle Bluff. It's also the most rewarding, with a myriad of picturesque little subalpine lakes and spectacular vistas from both Eagle Bluff and Black Mountain. The hike takes you into Nelson Canyon Park and along Whyte Creek, after which you join the original BP Trail heading up to Eagle Bluff and Black Mountain before descending to the Cypress Mountain ski area.

Note that with the completion of the new Highway 1/99 Eagleridge Bypass in 2009, it is possible to use the original Black Mountain trailhead again as an alternative (albeit a less desirable one) to the newer Nelson Canyon/Whyte Creek approach. You reach the former by taking the Eagleridge Exit 2 from Highway 1 in West Vancouver, then the first exit on the right from the round-about and pulling into a small, gravel parking area on your right a couple of minutes later. The Black Mountain Trail sign marks the trailhead, from which you walk up a gravel trail for about 5 minutes before going under the new Highway 99 overpass at Larson Creek. You then continue up the original BP Trail, along-side the highway at first, before soon heading into the forest.

This hike is best done in midsummer to early fall, long after the snow melts and before the fall rains start, as higher-level sections of the trail can be muddy and slippery in places.

From Highway 1 in West Vancouver, you reach the trailhead by taking Exit 4, then turning left onto Westport Road. Go straight through at the four-way stop and follow Westport Road for about 1½ kilometres (1 mile). Just after passing under the highway you see a Whyte Lake "P" for parking sign marking the small, gravel parking area off to the right. Arrange car transportation for both ends of this hike.

You begin by walking past the yellow gate, along the winding gravel road and under the highway. Keep going straight ahead for

Summertime at Cabin Lake.

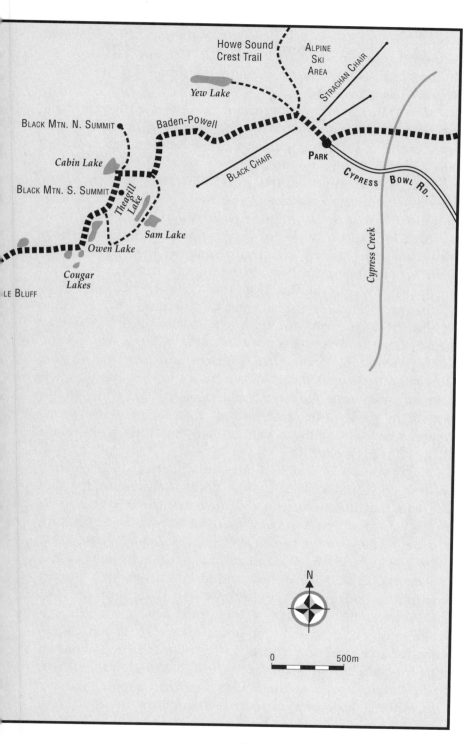

Howe Sound
Crest Trail

ALPINE
SKI
AREA

STRACHAN CHAIR

Yew Lake

BLACK MTN. N. SUMMIT

Baden-Powell

Cabin Lake

PARK

BLACK CHAIR

BLACK MTN. S. SUMMIT

CYPRESS BOWL RD.

Theagill Lake

Sam Lake

Cypress Creek

Owen Lake

Cougar
Lakes

LE BLUFF

N

0          500m

Whyte Lake at the first Trans Canada Trail (TCT) signpost, then turn right into the woods at a second TCT signpost a couple of minutes later. Following the winding uphill trail, you soon hear Nelson Creek on your left.

About 15 to 20 minutes from your car you leave the main trail by going down to your left at a signposted junction. In about 5 minutes this meandering trail leads to the Nelson Creek crossing on a sturdy footbridge built in 2008.

This recently improved trail now follows Whyte Creek west. After a series of three boardwalks you come to a signposted junction near Whyte Lake. Continue straight ahead up the slope then downhill for a couple of minutes to reach the signposted junction with the original BP route coming up from the old Eagleridge trailhead. Turn right here and head up the wide, rocky BP.

As it heads into the forest the trail gradually becomes more of a dirt path, crossing a small creek several times, then crossing Nelson Creek before beginning a steep ascent up the rock slide area. This part of the trail is not as well marked, but stay to your right, watching for orange flags on trees, small rock cairns and faint paint marks on boulders. As the grade steepens, carefully pick your way up among the large boulders. As you get closer to the top, still on the right-hand side, a dirt trail becomes more evident. You pass two false summits before finally reaching 1,094-metre (3,590-foot) Eagle Bluff.

Allow yourself 2½ to 3½ hours from your car to get to this point, a good lunch stop. The viewpoint is absolutely spectacular, with magnificent views across the entire Lower Mainland, as well as east to Mount Baker and south to Point Roberts. Looking down and west you see Eagle Lake, Eagle Harbour, Whyte Lake, Horseshoe Bay, over to Bowen Island and up the Sunshine Coast.

Leaving Eagle Bluff, follow the BP uphill into the woods, passing the Cougar Lakes and then Owen Lake, both on your right. The trail through this area can be muddy in places, although the installation of several long boardwalks in 2011 has greatly improved that situation. Shortly after Owen Lake and about an hour from Eagle Bluff, you reach the 1,217-metre (3,990-foot) Black Mountain south summit, a large rock outcropping on your right with a 360-degree panoramic view. From here continue north

Looking down to Eagle Lake and Eagle Harbour from Eagle Bluff.

and downhill about 190 metres (625 feet) on the dirt trail to the boardwalk and the signposted Cabin Lake junction. The very pretty Cabin Lake itself, a popular but cold swimming spot during the summer, is just over to your left.

From the junction you can also take a short side trip of about 250 metres (820 feet) north to the 1,224-metre (4,015-foot) Black Mountain north summit (a.k.a. Yew Lake Lookout), where you are treated to views of the Lions, the Sea to Sky Highway and as far north as the Tantalus Range.

Back at the junction take the boardwalk east for about 100 metres (330 feet) then turn left to follow the Baden-Powell "Ski Area Parking Lot" sign. This descent leads you down a fairly steep, switchbacking trail to the alpine ski area parking lot in 35 to 45 minutes.

# 18 ▸ Baden-Powell #2, Cypress Bowl to Cleveland Dam

**Elevation gain:** 150 metres (490 feet)
**High point:** 1,070 metres (3,500 feet)
**Season:** July to October
**Topographical map:** North Vancouver 92G06
**Hiking time:** 3½ to 4½ hours
Dog-friendly

After initially rising up to the Hollyburn Peak turnoff, this 12-kilo-metre (7½-mile) second segment of the Baden-Powell (BP) is almost all downhill. It takes you from the Cypress Mountain ski area to Cleveland Dam in North Vancouver. You descend through a variety of forested terrain, followed by a short trek across the top of the British Properties, then finally cross Cleveland Dam, where you are treated to views of Capilano Lake, the Lions and Grouse Mountain. (A midway access point is at upper Millstream Road in West Vancouver, reached by taking Exit 11 from Highway 1, going north on Crosscreek Road, left onto Chartwell Drive, then onto Millstream, staying left on Millstream to park just past Henlow Road.) It is best done in midsummer to early fall, long after the snow melts and before the fall rains start, as higher-level sections of the trail can be muddy and slippery in places.

From Highway 1 in West Vancouver you reach the trailhead by

taking Exit 8 for Cypress Park and following Cypress Bowl Road 14 kilometres (8½ miles) up to the alpine ski area parking lot. Arrange for car transportation to Cypress Bowl and either another car or public transit for the Cleveland Dam (or Millstream Road) end.

The Cypress Provincial Park trailhead signposts are located north of the parking lot and just past the Cypress Creek Lodge. As a shortcut for this hike, begin by taking the "Baden Powell Trail (Hollyburn Mountain)" direction on the signpost just behind the First Aid building. You go east and uphill on the ski run for a couple of minutes to where another signpost leads you into the woods. You now gradually gain elevation on an easy-to-follow, undulating forest path through large, second-growth fir and cedar. In the first half hour there is a crossing of a major Cypress Creek tributary that could be problematic if spring runoff levels are high.

Also, the trail is quite rooty, so is slippery when wet. There are some muddy patches as you approach the signposted Hollyburn Peak turnoff (see hike #8), about an hour from the start. Stay right at that junction, heading gradually downhill and alternating between forest cover and open areas.

After another 20 minutes or so you emerge into a clearing at

Hollyburn Lodge and First Lake from the Baden-Powell Trail.

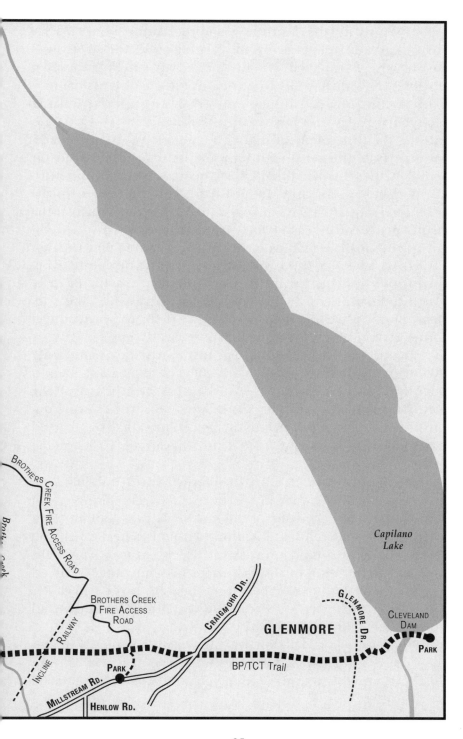

the power lines, with Fourth Lake and the warming hut on your right. Continue straight across the clearing under the power lines to follow the BP east and into the woods. Here you begin heading downhill on Upper Wells Gray, one of the major cross-country ski trails. In about 15 minutes you reach a bench overlooking Hollyburn Lodge and First Lake. Continue down the ski trail, passing the first couple of signposted junctions. After about 15 minutes from the bench you turn left at a signposted junction to follow the BP downhill on a short, narrow, rocky section, with views of Indian Arm and Mount Baker off to the east. From the open area, stay left at the signposted junction and left again at the orange marker on a tree to follow the BP into the woods.

Continuing downhill, you pass an access trail to Blue Gentian Lake (a possible side trip if you have some extra time; otherwise, see hike #10). About two hours from the start you reach a large clearing, the site of the former Westlake Ski Lodge, which was originally moved piecemeal from West Lake in 1938 but which burned to the ground over 20 years ago. Follow the BP sign left into the woods and continue downhill, passing a second, shorter—only 300 metres (980 feet)—access trail to Blue Gentian Lake. Soon to your right you hear Lawson Creek, which parallels the trail all the way down until you reach the power lines. Be wary of steep drop-offs in some places. Just before the power lines, take the marked trail to the left to pick up the BP/Trans Canada Trail (TCT) heading east.

Stay right on the BP/TCT at the Brothers Creek Trail junction, cross Brothers Creek, with its spectacular waterfall during spring runoff, and stay right again at the Incline Railway trail junction a few minutes later. About 20 minutes from Brothers Creek you reach a signposted junction with the fire access road. Stay right here and go downhill to another signposted junction at Hadden Creek, now about 3 to 3½ hours from the start. If you had earlier left a car at the upper Millstream Drive trailhead, take the trail down to the right and out to the road.

Otherwise, you go left, following the BP/TCT/Skyline Trail into the woods as it parallels the power lines east. At the Millstream Road/Craigmohr Drive intersection you go through a green metal

The Lions and Capilano Lake from Cleveland Dam.

gate to follow the BP east as it descends through the residential areas of the British Properties.

At Glenmore Drive, pick up the trail directly across the street as it heads into the woods again. There is a brief uphill followed by a fairly steep but short downhill before you emerge onto a gravel road. Go right here, following the winding gravel road all the way downhill until you reach Cleveland Dam, 40 minutes or so from the Hadden Creek junction. The parking lot and washrooms are just a couple of minutes ahead.

# 19 ► Baden-Powell #3, Grouse Mountain to Lynn Canyon

> **Elevation gain:** 216 metres (700 feet)
> **High point:** 490 metres (1,600 feet)
> **Season:** April to November
> **Topographical map:** North Vancouver 92G06
> **Hiking time:** 3¼ to 4 hours
> Dog-friendly

You will find this third, and, at just over 10 kilometres (6¼ miles), shortest segment of the Baden-Powell (BP), through second-growth forest along the lower slopes of Grouse Mountain and Mount Fromme, to be quite rewarding, particularly from Mosquito Creek east. There are lots of ups and downs along the way, but no major elevation gains, and many sections of upgraded trail. Although the last segment ended at Cleveland Dam, we will forgo the 2-kilometre (1¼-mile) trek from the dam up Nancy Greene Way and start at the base of the Grouse Mountain Skyride (at the start of the Grouse Grind), finishing at the Lynn Canyon Park suspension bridge. (A midway access point is at the top of St. Marys Avenue, reached by driving north on Lonsdale Avenue from Highway 1, turning right on Braemar Road, left on St. Georges Avenue, and right on Wooddale Road to park anywhere on Wooddale or on St. Marys below Wooddale.)

From Highway 1 in North Vancouver, take Exit 14 to go north on Capilano Road. Follow it past Cleveland Dam and up Nancy Greene Way to the free gravel parking lot on your right (or the pay lot on your left) as you approach the Grouse Mountain Skyride. Arrange either car or public transit for both ends of this hike.

Begin by heading uphill and east from the trailhead gate, passing the Grouse Grind turnoff on your left, followed by a BCMC (British Columbia Mountaineering Club) turnoff (see hike #22) about 5 minutes later. You continue steadily uphill on the BP for the next 20 to 30 minutes before the trail levels out somewhat. Over the next half hour or so you pass two more signposted junctions for the old BCMC Trail and cross two tributaries of MacKay Creek (without footbridges, so take care if water levels are high). A little over an hour from the start and about 10 minutes after passing a signposted junction for the 150-metre (490-foot) trail that goes down to Skyline Drive, you follow the BP signs down to a major footbridge across the sometimes-tumultuous Mosquito Creek canyon.

Looking north up Lynn Creek from the Baden-Powell Trail.

Immediately after the bridge, there is a signposted junction for the 250-metre (820-foot) trail that goes down to Prospect Road, but you follow the BP left and uphill, passing two large, green water towers on your right. About 20 minutes from Mosquito Creek and 1½ hours from the start you come to a bench with a fine view of Burrard Inlet, Vancouver and beyond.

If you had earlier left a car at St. Marys, you now take the St. Georges Trail down to your right about 10 metres (30 feet) past the bench. Follow the red markers on the trees for about 10 minutes downhill until you emerge at the power lines. Here you go left and almost immediately you see ahead the gate at the top of St. Marys. Just past this gate, go to your right and downhill on St. Marys to your car.

Otherwise, continue your trek east along this very pleasant section of the BP on your way to Lynn Canyon, passing many well-marked intersections with Mount Fromme mountain bike trails on your way. About 25 minutes past Kilmer Creek and perhaps 2½ hours from the start you emerge onto Mountain Highway (now the old Grouse Mountain Highway at this point), with its welcome water fountain and places to sit. Pick up the BP directly across the road and follow the signs downhill, eventually going down several flights of stairs, to reach the Lynn Headwaters access road about 20 minutes after leaving Mountain Highway.

Go right here and follow this road for about 15 minutes out to the stop sign at the Lynn Valley Road/Dempsey Road intersection. Go to your left at the BP signpost near the "Fire Warning" sign, following the dirt trail down into Lynn Canyon. This winding path leads you south along the west side of Lynn Creek, with several boardwalks and stairs along the way, before you reach the suspension bridge about 20 minutes from the last intersection. Go up the stairs to your right to reach the Lynn Canyon Ecology Centre, Lynn Canyon Café, washrooms and the parking area.

# 20 ► Baden-Powell #4, Lynn Canyon to Deep Cove

**Elevation gain:** 380 metres (1,240 feet)
**High point:** 430 metres (1,400 feet)
**Season:** April to November
**Topographical map:** North Vancouver 92G06 and
Port Coquitlam 92G07
**Hiking time:** 3½ to 4½ hours
Dog-friendly

This fourth and final segment of the Baden-Powell (BP) Trail, at just over 12 kilometres (7½ miles), takes you across two impressive river canyons, the Lynn and the Seymour. It also includes one of the BP's more strenuous uphill sections, followed by a very satisfying downhill ramble toward a Deep Cove lookout point, with lots of creeks and footbridges the rest of the way. The hike starts at the Lynn Canyon Park suspension bridge and finishes at Deep Cove. (A midway access point is at Hyannis Drive, reached by taking Exit 22 from Highway 1 in North Vancouver, going east on Mount Seymour Parkway, turning left onto Berkley Road and left again onto Hyannis at the top of Berkley.)

From Highway 1 in North Vancouver, take Exit 19 to go north on Lynn Valley Road. Soon after the shopping centre and the lights at Mountain Highway you pass a Royal Bank, then turn right on Peters Road to enter Lynn Canyon Park. Arrange either car or public transit for both ends of this hike.

You begin at the BP signpost on the west side of the suspension bridge. Cross the bridge, go along the boardwalk and follow the BP to the right toward the Twin Falls Bridge, where you may see cliff jumpers in the summer months. Take a minute to admire the view of the falls, then continue south along the east side of Lynn Creek. This is a winding dirt trail, rooty in places, but with several boardwalks. About 10 minutes from Twin Falls, partway along an elevated boardwalk, there is a nice little beach just off to your right.

Shortly after that boardwalk you begin your climb out of Lynn Canyon. About 10 to 15 minutes later you reach a BP signposted junction at the top of the hill. Go left to follow the BP northeast to Lillooet Road. Pick up the trail across the road and continue southeast toward the Seymour River, passing the Richard Juryn Trail signposts (see hike #28). A few minutes later carefully follow the switchbacking trail downhill, then descend a steep flight of

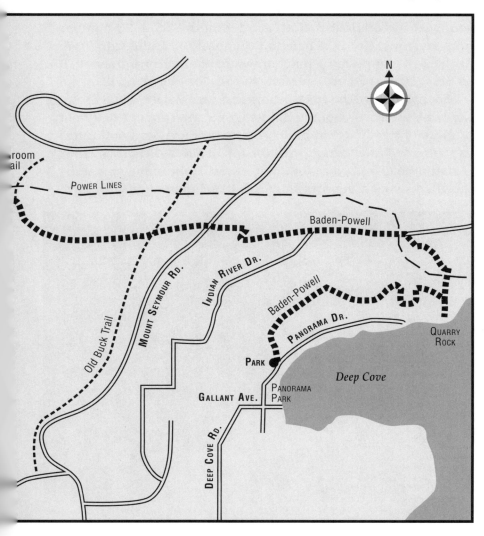

stairs to the pipe bridge over the canyon. After a short uphill on the other side, you see a footbridge out to Riverside Drive on your right, but you turn left to follow the BP north. At a signposted junction with the Fisherman's Trail a couple of minutes later, go right and follow the BP alongside Canyon Creek up to Hyannis Drive.

Arriving at Hyannis, about 1¼ to 1½ hours from the suspension bridge, pick up the BP on the other side of the road (unless you had earlier left a car here in order to complete this segment another day). Continue along the creek, going steadily uphill until you meet the Bridle Path Trail at a footbridge 15 to 20 minutes from Hyannis. Go right here, on the joint BP/Bridle Path Trail. At the next signposted T-junction where the trails part, about 70 metres (230 feet) ahead, you turn left to follow the BP north.

Soon you leave the creek behind and the BP starts a fairly steep climb, not unlike part of the Grouse Grind. After about a half hour or more of steady uphill plodding the trail levels out a bit near its signposted intersection with the top of Severed D (a.k.a. Good Samaritan), a good place for a water stop. Continuing east along the BP for about 5 minutes you reach its signposted junction with

Baden-Powell Trail between Mount Seymour Road and Indian River Drive.

the Mushroom Parking Lot trail (a possible side trip if you have an extra half hour or so; otherwise, see hike #32). Continue east along the BP until you reach its junction with Old Buck Trail, an old logging road used by the Buck's Logging Company in the 1920s. Turn left up Old Buck for about 80 metres (260 feet), then right to continue east on the BP. This section of the BP is a pleasant, winding forest path that heads gradually downhill for the next few minutes until it emerges at Mount Seymour Road, about 1¼ to 1½ hours from Hyannis.

Pick up the BP directly across the road and follow this very agreeable trail until you reach Indian River Drive. Here you go left and walk along the road for 500 metres (one-third mile), passing under power lines just before reaching the BP signpost on your right. Take this trail downhill and back into the forest. In about 5 minutes you reach a wide dirt road; continue straight ahead across the road to follow the BP downhill at the signpost. After another 5 minutes or so you come out at the power lines again. Continue south directly across the open space and just to the right of the transmission tower to pick up the BP as it heads downhill.

In another couple of minutes you see Quarry Rock, sometimes referred to as Grey Rock, in a clearing directly ahead of you. A hundred years ago Granite Quarries Ltd. was located just below this lookout, and operated from 1908 to 1924. Take a break here to enjoy the spectacular, 180-degree views of Deep Cove, Indian Arm and beyond. When you're ready to continue, take the BP Trail out to your left (west). At a steady pace you reach Deep Cove and the end of the 48-kilometre (30-mile) Baden-Powell Trail in about half an hour.

# NORTH VANCOUVER

## 21 ▶ Capilano Canyon

**Elevation gain:** minimal
**High point:** 150 metres (490 feet)
**Season:** Year-round
**Topographical map:** North Vancouver 92G06
**Hiking time:** 2½ to 3½ hours
Dog-friendly

Here is an all-weather jaunt that provides a comprehensive introduction to both the popular and the less-travelled trails of Capilano River Regional Park, including visits to the Capilano River Fish Hatchery and some giant old-growth Douglas firs. The hike takes you from Cleveland Dam down the west side of the Capilano River, across the river for a loop down the lesser-known east side, then back up to the hatchery and across the river again for your return to Cleveland Dam. There are several opportunities along the way to shorten the hike, depending on how much time you have.

From Highway 1 in North Vancouver, take Exit 14 to go north on Capilano Road. Follow it up to the paved parking lot on your left, just past Clements Avenue but before Nancy Greene Way heads up toward Grouse Mountain. This lovely, 160-hectare

(395-acre) park was created in 1926 and is administered by Metro Vancouver. The river was originally known as Homulchesan, as was the native village at its mouth. It was later renamed after the great Squamish chief Kia'palano, who died about 1875 and was buried on the Mission Reserve in North Vancouver.

Begin by walking across Cleveland Dam, admiring the views of Capilano Lake, the Lions and Grouse Mountain up on your right, then the awe-inspiring spillway and vertical canyon walls to your left. The dam was completed in 1954 and named after Ernest A. Cleveland, the first chief commissioner of the Greater Vancouver Water District from 1926 to 1952. Across the dam you see two gravel roads on your left. The lower one will be your return route, so take the upper one with the BP (Baden-Powell Trail) signplate.

Follow the BP uphill, turning left in about 5 minutes at the signposted Shinglebolt Trail junction. Take the Shinglebolt down-hill, going left at the bottom of the wooden steps. About 40 metres (130 feet) farther on go right up a short tangle of tree roots. Next you turn right down a wooden staircase, and follow red markers on the trees down a short trail. Go right at the bench, then down some stairs to a signposted junction with the Capilano Pacific Trail (see hike #16).

Go right here and cross the reinforced footbridge over Houlgate Creek. The creek was named after R.K. Houlgate, a Vancouver Board of Trade member and part of a syndicate that constructed a long, wooden flume to transport shingle bolts (long, wedge-shaped blocks of cedar from which shakes and shingles were cut) from a steam sawmill at Sisters Creek, a tributary of the Capilano, all the way down the river to Burrard Inlet in the early 1900s.

Continue south for 10 to 15 minutes following the scenic Capilano Pacific, the route of the 8½-kilometre (5.3-mile) Coho Walk each September from Cleveland Dam to Ambleside Park in West Vancouver, until you reach an observation platform on your left with a dramatic view of the canyon. From the lookout return back upstream to the Houlgate Creek bridge.

After crossing the bridge, follow the Capilano Pacific along to a signposted junction where you go right, down the Shinglebolt Trail and across a gravel road to reach the Pipeline Bridge river crossing. On the other side, take the Chinook Trail up to your right and follow it south as it parallels the river. Five to ten minutes later, at a Trans Canada Trail signpost, you can take a short, dirt side trail down to a sunny, level but rocky area next to the river. Returning to the main trail, about 10 minutes later you reach a yellow gate that marks the junction of the Chinook Trail with

Capilano Park Road and the Pipeline Trail. Go left here to follow the gravel Pipeline Trail back north into the woods.

Emerging at the Pipeline Bridge junction again, go right to take the Coho Loop Trail as it winds its way north along the east side of the river canyon, passing the Cable Pool on the way. Next you see the Cable Pool Bridge ahead on your left. Leaving this for the moment, stay to the right to visit the fish hatchery and take in its educational displays and check for activity in its fish ladders.

If you are short of time, the Palisades Trail just east of the hatchery provides a convenient, albeit fairly steep, one-kilometre (half-mile) shortcut back up to the parking lot. Otherwise, return to cross the Cable Pool Bridge, watching downstream for fishermen trying their luck in the deep pools below.

Across the bridge, turn right and follow this trail upstream for about 5 minutes to the Second Canyon Viewpoint lookout area, with its spectacular view of the dam spillway. There are also story-boards that outline the early history of the canyon and identify the various salmon species that use the river and the hatchery fish ladders. From here retrace your steps about 60 metres (200 feet) and take the Giant Fir Trail to your right and uphill. In the next

Fishing in the Capilano River Cable Pool, downstream from the Cable Pool Bridge.

5 minutes or so you pass two massive old-growth Douglas firs, 2.3 metres (7½ feet) and 1.8 metres (6 feet) in diameter. Finally you reach the ancient Grandpa Capilano, which at 2.4 metres (8 feet) in diameter and more than 60 metres (200 feet) high is the largest remaining Douglas fir in the park, and believed to be more than 800 years old.

Continue up this trail, turning right at its junction with the Capilano Pacific a few minutes later. Now follow that trail on its gradual ascent up to Cleveland Dam and return to the parking lot.

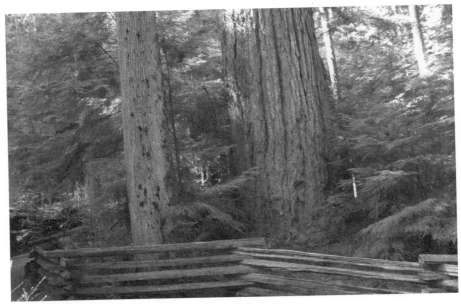

The "Grandpa Capilano" Douglas fir in Capilano Canyon.

# 22 ► Grouse Mountain– Lower Fromme Round Trip

**Elevation gain:** 850 metres (2,800 feet)
**High point:** 1,125 metres (3,700 feet)
**Season:** July to October
**Topographical map:** North Vancouver 92G06
**Hiking time:** 5 to 6 hours, including lunch
Dogs not permitted on Grouse Mountain Resorts Ltd. property

Here is a lengthy, moderately strenuous but rewarding trek that introduces you to two of North Vancouver's most prominent mountains. The hike takes you up Grouse Mountain on the BC Mountaineering Club (BCMC) Trail, then down along the old Grouse Mountain Highway (GMH) toward Mount Fromme, the lower slopes of which you skirt via the GMH, Per Gynt and St. Georges trails before descending to the Baden-Powell (BP) Trail for your return to the start.

From Highway 1 in North Vancouver, take Exit 14 to go north on Capilano Road. Follow it past Cleveland Dam and up Nancy Greene Way to the free gravel parking lot on your right (or the paved pay lot on your left) as you approach the Grouse Mountain Skyride.

Begin by heading uphill and east from the trailhead gate, passing the Grouse Grind turnoff on your left before reaching the marked start of the BCMC Trail about 5 minutes later. Many hikers find the BCMC Trail an attractive alternative to the Grind; it is a slightly longer, but more gradual approach to the top, and much quieter than the often-crowded "Mother Nature's Stairmaster."

The elevation gain is the same, and you should plan on one to two hours, depending on your fitness level. Ample water is a must, particularly in hot weather.

The BCMC Trail is quite easy to follow, with its "BCMC" markers on the trees all the way up, conveniently numbered from 1 to 152. This somewhat rocky, rooty trail climbs steadily, then begins to level out a bit around marker #120, an hour or so from the start.

Nearing the top, you reach a signed trail junction a few minutes after marker #122. Take the "Pipeline" route to the left rather than the "Sunview" to the right, to avoid ending up too far east of the Peak Chalet. A few minutes later, turn left on a wide gravel trail, then follow an obvious waterline uphill for another couple of minutes to emerge just east of the Grind and at the back of the chalet, with its washrooms and food facilities.

Next, follow the signs from the front of the chalet up to the grizzly bear habitat that houses Coola and Grinder, two orphan grizzlies. After watching these fascinating creatures for a few minutes, make your way over to the Peak Office building with its Rusty Rail BBQ and public washrooms before leaving Grouse for Fromme.

Now follow the gravel road south from the Peak Office. It winds around to the left as it reaches The Cut (with its Screaming Eagle chair on your right), and initially heads north, then starts switchbacking down the side of Grouse. Several dirt roads branch off the GMH, but stay on this main wide gravel road as it heads generally northeast. Looking over to Mount Fromme, you can see the GMH continuing along its lower slopes.

Grouse Mountain Resorts Ltd. owns the upper part of the Grouse Mountain Highway from between the fifth and sixth switchbacks, and does not endorse the use of it for hiking. There is regular vehicle traffic on this highway and use of it is entirely at the hiker's own risk. Grouse Mountain Resorts Ltd. takes no responsibility for loss or injury incurred by anyone using this highway.

In about three-quarters of an hour, you pass the Grouse Mountain Resorts Ltd. "Private Road" sign on a tree to your left. About 20 metres (65 feet) past the sign you may notice a flagged

Mount Fromme and, in the background, the Needles, from the old Grouse Mountain Highway.

trail going into the woods on your left. This Pipeline Pass route, which follows an old wooden pipeline part of the way, leads north toward Thunderbird Ridge.

Continuing along the GMH, in 15 minutes or so you see another flagged trail on your left. This is the upper Per Gynt approach to Mount Fromme (as described in hike #23). In about another 15 minutes, just after passing a gravel pit on your left, you reach a signposted junction on your right indicating the top part of the lower Per Gynt Trail. Take this trail downhill into the woods to avoid a large switchback of the GMH, which you rejoin 10 to 12 minutes later.

Follow the GMH again for 3 or 4 minutes, passing the sign-posted Executioner mountain bike trail start, before taking the signposted St. Georges Trail down to your right. Watch your footing on the loose rocks as you head downhill on the St. Georges for another 20 minutes or so to its intersection with the BP. Here you can appreciate a few minutes rest on a comfortable bench with a fine view over to Vancouver.

Continuing a pleasant trek west from the bench along the BP, you pass the Executioner Trail exit then two large, green water towers on your left before reaching Mosquito Creek 20 to 25 minutes from the bench.

After crossing the sturdy Mosquito Creek footbridge and following the BP signs partway up the hill, passing two houses on your left, there are two possibilities for your return to the start. If you are short of time, instead of following the BP signpost up and to the right, you can go left and follow a paved driveway downhill to Skyline Drive. In a couple of minutes you reach an information kiosk, then follow along the open Power Lines Trail all the way to the parking lot in another 20 to 25 minutes.

Otherwise, follow the BP back uphill and continue along, crossing two tributaries of MacKay Creek (without footbridges, so take care if water levels are high) about 5 minutes apart. About 10 minutes past MacKay Creek West, the trail starts going generally downhill. You pass the BCMC Trail junction about 15 minutes later before reaching the trailhead gate near the parking lot about an hour from Mosquito Creek.

# 23 ▶ Mount Fromme

**Elevation gain:** 820 metres (2,690 feet)
**High point (south peak):** 1,186 metres (3,890 feet)
**Season:** July to October
**Topographical map:** North Vancouver 92G06
**Hiking time:** 5½ to 6½ hours, including lunch
Dog-friendly

Mount Fromme offers excellent viewpoints from both of its peaks. Numerous approaches to Grouse Mountain's overlooked neighbour to the east have been documented over the years; this one is an energetic, satisfying combination of old and new. Starting from the top of St. Marys Avenue in North Vancouver, this challenging but rewarding hike takes you up the St. Georges Trail to the old Grouse Mountain Highway (GMH), then alternates between the GMH and Per Gynt Trail segments to its conclusion at Mount Fromme's twin summits and Meech Lake. For some additional variety, Bill's Trail provides a very pleasant alternative on the way down.

Mount Fromme is named for Julius Martin Fromme, a prominent early North Vancouver settler. Known as the father of Lynn Valley, Fromme owned the Lynn Valley Lumber Company in the early 1900s and was district reeve for seven terms.

From Highway 1 in North Vancouver, take Exit 18 for Lonsdale Avenue. Going north on Lonsdale, turn right on Braemar Road,

left on St. Georges Avenue and right on Wooddale Road to park anywhere on Wooddale or on St. Marys below Wooddale.

Begin by walking north on St. Marys, then going left at the Power Lines Trail to head west. A couple of minutes past the Skid Road mountain bike trail signpost, take the signposted St. Georges Trail up to your right. About 15 minutes from the start, just after crossing the Dreamweaver mountain bike trail, the St. Georges intersects the Baden-Powell (BP) near a comfortable bench. Here you cross the BP and continue up the St. Georges. This trail is fairly steep, with lots of gravel and loose rock, but is easy to follow.

In 25 minutes or so, passing one or two intersections with biking trails, you reach a signposted junction with the old GMH. Turn left to follow this wide, gravel road west for less than 5 minutes until it makes a sharp, right-hand turn. Here you take the signposted Per Gynt Trail into the woods on your left, following it roughly north-northeast uphill, effectively avoiding a large switch-back of the GMH before emerging on it again about 15 minutes later.

Go left to follow the road leading generally north, passing a large gravel pit on your right in a couple of minutes. To your left is Grouse Mountain (see hike #22), with the GMH intersecting its Blueberry Bowl ski runs, and its Eye of the Wind turbine higher up on the peak. About 20 minutes from the lower Per Gynt, just after passing a wide, rocky ravine, watch for orange flags hanging in the trees on your right, indicating the start of the upper Per Gynt.

This dirt trail, while not well maintained, has frequent orange ribbons and metal markers on the trees making it quite easy to follow as it climbs steadily uphill. It is steep and scrambly in places, with lots of roots and rocks along the way, so is best done in dry weather. After about 45 minutes or so and nearly 300 metres (985 feet) of elevation gain, the trail levels off somewhat into a very pleasant subalpine area with more views west toward Grouse Mountain.

Continuing east along the marked trail for about 5 minutes, you reach a well-marked, four-way trail junction. On your right is Bill's Trail (your route back down to the GMH); to your left is part of the "Main Trail," which can take you down to the quite pretty and peaceful Meech Lake in about 5 minutes. Just a couple of minutes straight ahead and to the left, you reach the open part of the south summit, which offers views east to Lynn Peak (see hike #26), the Needles and Coliseum Mountain, while overlooking Lynn Creek and the third debris chute on the Lynn Headwaters Trail.

From the south summit, follow the sign to Senate Peak (the north summit), going down steeply at first then up again to the rocky peak in 5 to 10 minutes. Senate Peak, although the lower of the two by about 16 metres (52 feet), has a nice open area for a lunch break, and the better viewpoints. Looking south and west, you see English Bay, Grouse Mountain and Crown Mountain; on a perfectly clear day you can see north to Mount Garibaldi.

Leaving the north summit you see on your right another "Main Trail" sign, which would lead you down a steep descent to Pipeline Pass and eventually the GMH (passing a junction with the other part of the "Main Trail" from Meech Lake on the way). Leaving that option for another day, retrace your steps back to the

Grouse Mountain's Blueberry Bowl ski runs and the old Grouse Mountain Highway from Mount Fromme's north peak.

south summit, and from there to the junction with Bill's Trail, the upper Per Gynt and the trail to Meech Lake.

For your return, take the more gradual Bill's Trail, a well-maintained route heading roughly south down the mountain, parallel to the GMH for much of the way, and avoiding the steep descent of the upper Per Gynt.

In about an hour or so, Bill's Trail emerges onto the GMH, almost directly across from the signposted top of the lower Per Gynt segment. Follow the Per Gynt downhill for 10 to 12 minutes to connect again with the GMH, which you follow for 3 or 4 minutes, passing the signposted Executioner mountain bike trail start, to reach its signposted junction with the St. Georges Trail. Watch your footing on the loose rocks as you head downhill on the St. Georges for another 20 minutes or so to its intersection with the BP.

Here you may appreciate a few minutes rest on the bench before continuing another 10 minutes down the St. Georges to the power lines, then left to St. Marys and down to your car.

Descending to pretty Meech Lake on Mount Fromme.

# 24 ▶ St. Marys/Dempsey/ Baden-Powell Loop

**Elevation gain:** 180 metres (590 feet)
**High point:** 490 metres (1,600 feet)
**Season:** April to November
**Topographical map:** North Vancouver 92G06
**Hiking time:** 2 to 2½ hours
Dog-friendly

This rewarding little outing, with only moderate elevation gain, introduces you to one of the Baden-Powell (BP) Trail's most pleasant sections, as well as the lesser-known but quite delightful St. Marys Trail, along the lower slopes of Mount Fromme. Starting from the trailhead on St. Marys Avenue, it takes you east along the St. Marys, onto the Dempsey Trail, then up to the BP via the Quarry Court Trail. Heading back west along the BP, you descend back to St. Marys on either one of two return routes.

From Highway 1 in North Vancouver, take Exit 18 for Lonsdale Avenue. Going north on Lonsdale, turn right on Braemar Road, left on St. Georges Avenue and right on Wooddale Road to park anywhere on Wooddale or on St. Marys below Wooddale.

Begin by walking about 35 metres (115 feet) down St. Marys from Wooddale, then go left at the St. Marys Trail entrance to head northeast. The trail begins as a wide, fairly level, gravel path as you approach the power lines. Crossing under the power lines, you head north uphill and into the woods, where the trail becomes a little more rocky and rooty. This undulating trail is well marked and easy to follow as you head generally east now, passing several signposted junctions with mountain bike trails.

In 15 to 20 minutes from the start, a signpost tells you that the St. Marys Trail is now the Dempsey Trail. Continuing straight

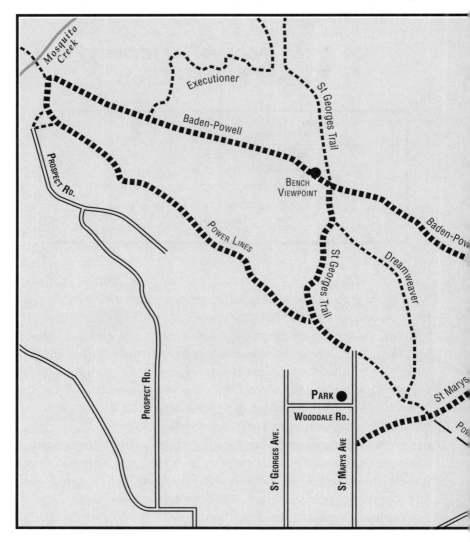

ahead, in another 5 minutes or so the Dempsey becomes the Dempsey Connector, with a residential area (E. Braemar Road) just through the trees on your right. About half an hour from the start you cross Kilmer Creek, then reach the Kilmer mountain bike trail junction. Continuing straight ahead, you cross another couple of small creeks over the next few minutes. This part of the trail is not as well marked, but still well travelled and quite easy to follow.

About 10 minutes from Kilmer Creek, and just after passing the

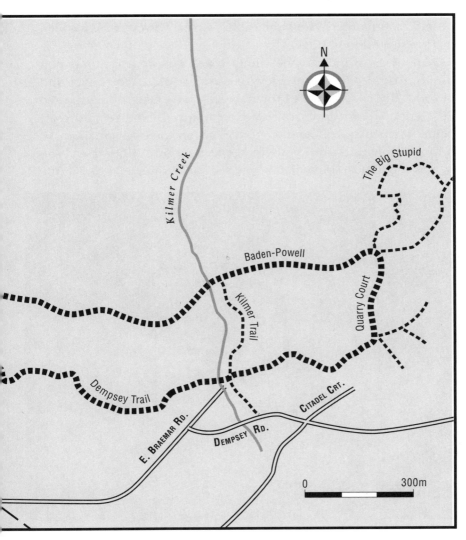

Citadel Court residential area through some bushes on your right, you come to the signposted Quarry Court Trail junction. Here you go up to your left on this hiking-only trail to meet up with the BP. After 10 minutes or so of fairly steady ascent, you reach the signposted junction with the BP (and the exit of the Big Stupid mountain bike trail). Turning right here would take you east along the BP to where it crosses Mountain Highway in about 15 minutes (see hike #19), but for today you go left to follow the BP west. Another 10 minutes or so takes you to one more crossing of the Kilmer mountain bike trail and Kilmer Creek, with its nice wooden boardwalk and footbridge.

About 25 minutes from Kilmer Creek you approach a bench on your right with a fine view of Burrard Inlet, Vancouver and beyond. If you are short of time you can now take the signposted St. Georges Trail down to your left about 10 metres (30 feet) before the bench. Follow the red markers on the trees for about 10 minutes downhill until you emerge at the power lines. Here you go left and almost immediately you see ahead the metal gate at the

Some late winter snow on the Baden-Powell footbridge over Kilmer Creek.

top of St. Marys Avenue. Just past this gate, go to your right and downhill on St. Marys to your car.

Otherwise, continue west along the very pleasant BP toward Mosquito Creek, which you will begin to hear in about 20 minutes from the bench, 10 minutes or so after passing the signposted Executioner mountain bike trail exit.

Rather than descending to the Mosquito Creek crossing, go down to your left at the BP/Prospect Road signpost to reach the power lines area in just a couple of minutes. Follow the trail to your left (not down to Prospect Road), as it takes you through the bush for a few metres, then out into the open, where it leads you gradually uphill and southeast along the power lines. In 15 to 20 minutes you pass the Skid Road mountain bike trail signpost on your left, and then reach the metal gate at the top of St. Marys a couple of minutes later.

A raging torrent on the St. Marys Trail.

# 25 ▶ Norvan Falls

**Elevation gain:** 190 metres (620 feet)
**High point:** 370 metres (1,200 feet)
**Season:** May to November
**Topographical map:** North Vancouver 92G06
**Hiking time:** 4 to 5 hours, including lunch
Dog-friendly

This rewarding, 14- to 15-kilometre (8½- to 9-mile) return trip through the lush rainforest of Lynn Headwaters Regional Park features only gradual elevation changes along the way to the impressive Norvan Falls. The hike takes you along a route with abundant evidence of early 1900s' logging activities to a viewpoint below Norvan Falls, then back to the trailhead either directly or via a somewhat longer Lynn Loop Trail circuit.

From Highway 1 in North Vancouver, take Exit 19 to go north on Lynn Valley Road. After passing a shopping centre then the lights at Mountain Highway, watch for signs for Lynn Headwaters Park (passing the turnoff for Lynn Canyon Park) and park in the small paved lot at the end of the access road or in either of the two overflow lots. The park is administered by Metro Vancouver and was reopened to the public in 1985 after being closed since 1928 as part of the North Shore watershed system.

Begin by taking the footbridge across Lynn Creek and going

Norvan Falls.

left at the trailhead kiosk (the trail coming down from the right is your Lynn Loop return route). On this wide, gravel Cedars Mill Trail you see occasional remnants of logging activity, such as an old four-wheeled log transporter at the half-kilometre mark, more rusted machinery at the signposted Cedars Mill site and of course the ubiquitous massive old-growth stumps.

After 20 to 25 minutes along this very pleasant trail you reach a short connector path up to the Lynn Loop/Headwaters Trail, but continue to your left, following Lynn Creek north. At the end of a boardwalk, stay straight ahead rather than going up the stairs to the right. The trail now narrows and becomes rougher and more winding, but is still very easy to follow, even without the yellow markers on the trees. At about 4 kilometres (2½ miles), 45 minutes or so from the start, you reach a large clearing and debris chute. The nearby Mount Fromme (see hike #23) towers up to the west and the creek access here provides a good spot for a break.

Continue north, now on the Headwaters Trail, from the signpost at the top of the debris chute. Soon you see stretches of the deteriorating old corduroy logging road and cookhouse relics from a logging camp of a century ago. The trail now becomes a little steeper and rockier in places, but is also farther from the creek, so you are truly in the peace and quiet of the forest.

About 40 to 50 minutes from the debris chute you pass the signposted turnoff to your right for the Coliseum Mountain hike. This 7-hour trip has over 1,000 metres (3,300 feet) more elevation gain and is suitable only for experienced and well-prepared hikers. Just ahead you reach Norvan Creek. The steel suspension bridge leads north to a very rugged trail to Lynn Lake, again suitable only for experienced and well-prepared hikers, or to the challenging Hanes Valley crossover route to Grouse Mountain, with another 1,000 metres (3,300 feet) elevation gain and roughly another 6 hours one way. For today, take the short access trail about 5 minutes upstream and find a creekside lunchtime viewpoint of the dramatic, 20-metre-high (65-foot) Norvan Falls.

To begin your return trip, retrace your steps back to the debris chute. For a little more variety, stay left at the signpost to continue on the upper Headwaters Trail rather than returning via the lower Cedars Mill Trail. The upper trail is about twice as long

An old, four-wheeled log transporter from the early 1900s.

and somewhat rougher than the lower one, but is also more like a continuation of the woodsy, peaceful trail from Norvan Creek to this point.

About 35 to 45 minutes from the debris chute, you reach the signposted junction with the switchback connector path down to the Cedars Mill Trail, another option for your return if you are running short of time. Otherwise, continue along what is now the upper part of the Lynn Loop Trail, an interesting stretch punctuated by little creeks and footbridges, and surrounded by many more old-growth stumps.

In another half hour or so you pass the signposted turnoff to the Lynn Peak trail (see hike #26) on your left. From here the Lynn Loop Trail continues its descent for another few minutes, now as a wide gravel path, before meeting the connector trail from Rice Lake in the Lower Seymour Conservation Reserve (see hike #27). Go downhill to your right for another 5 minutes to the trailhead kiosk, where you cross the footbridge back to the parking lot.

# 26 ► Lynn Peak and Lynn Loop

> **Elevation gain:** 803 metres (2,630 feet)
> **High point:** 983 metres (3,220 feet)
> **Season:** June to October
> **Topographical map:** North Vancouver 92G06
> **Hiking time:** 4½ to 5½ hours, including lunch
> Dog-friendly (but no water on Lynn Peak)

Anyone heading north across the Ironworkers Memorial Bridge cannot miss the prominent Lynn Peak, in Lynn Headwaters Regional Park, straight ahead. Lynn Peak, Lynn Creek and the other "Lynns" were named (misspelled) after the Scottish Royal Engineers sapper John Linn, who established a homestead with his family just east of the creek's mouth in 1869. This hike will provide a good cardio workout on the way up, without the crowds of the Grouse Grind, and some great, rewarding views from the top on a clear day. The Lynn Loop Trail offers a very attractive one-hour alternative, with minimal additional elevation gain, for your return route.

From Highway 1 in North Vancouver, take Exit 19 to go north on Lynn Valley Road. After passing the Lynn Valley shopping centre, the intersection with Mountain Highway and the Royal Bank, watch for signs for Lynn Headwaters Park (passing the turnoff for Lynn Canyon Park) and park in the small paved lot at the end of the access road, or in either of the two overflow lots.

You begin by taking the footbridge across Lynn Creek and going right up a wide, gravel road from the trailhead kiosk (the trail coming in from the left is your Lynn Loop return route). In about 5 minutes you reach a large signpost marking the boundary between Lynn Headwaters and the Lower Seymour Conservation

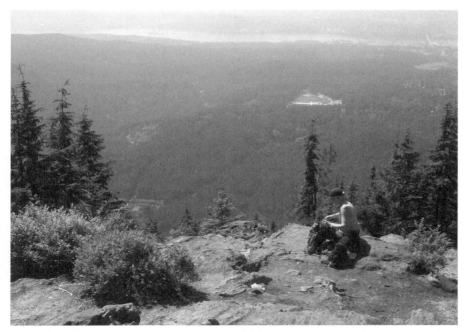

The Lynn Peak viewpoint overlooking North Vancouver, Burrard Inlet and beyond.

Reserve. Continuing straight ahead here would take you to Rice Lake (see hike #27), but you go up to your left, following the wide, gravel Lynn Loop Trail as it winds gradually uphill, passing many giant, old-growth stumps, stark remnants of the early 1900s' logging in the area.

In 15 to 20 minutes from the start you come to the Lynn Loop's signposted junction with the Lynn Peak Trail. Noting the 6.4-kilometre (4-mile) round-trip distance, you go right to begin your trek up to Lynn Peak.

Follow the yellow square markers on the trees as this well-used but rough trail, with lots of rocks and roots, switchbacks steadily uphill. The trail is fairly steep most of the way up, although it does level out a bit in a few places. One of these spots is your first minor viewpoint, an eastern outlook to Mount Seymour, 35 to 40 minutes from the Lynn Peak Trail junction.

The trail levels out to another flat stretch about 15 minutes later, as it leads through a stand of lovely old-growth trees known as the "Enchanted Forest." In particular, watch on your left for a huge western red cedar and an even larger Douglas fir.

In another 10 to 15 minutes you reach a second viewpoint, an open area just off the trail on the east side of the ridge, known as the "Blimp Lookout" after the dirigible moored here in a 1960s balloon logging operation attempting to recover some of the timber damaged by Hurricane Frieda in 1962. Looking over to Mount Seymour in the east again, you have a fine view of Dog Mountain (see hike #36) and the very steep Suicide Bluffs.

After another short uphill section of 15 to 20 minutes, and 1½ to 2 hours from the start, you reach the peak, with its large, open area on your right, a little below the summit itself. Here you are treated to spectacular views of a heavily forested portion of North Vancouver far below you. Pretty little Rice Lake is nestled in the trees just north of the large Seymour-Capilano water filtration plant area, with the winding Seymour River to the east and the Ironworkers Memorial Bridge spanning Burrard Inlet to the southwest.

Once you have rested a while and perhaps had some lunch, start your descent, remembering to watch your footing on the steeper parts with loose rocks or wet, slippery tree roots.

Upon reaching the Lynn Peak/Lynn Loop Trail junction you have two options for your return route. The shorter of the two (about 15 minutes and 1.2 kilometres or three-quarters of a mile back) is to go left and continue retracing your steps back down the way you came up.

Otherwise, if you have an extra hour or so, go right to follow the Lynn Loop Trail north (4 kilometres or 2½ miles back). This trail starts off as a fine, gravel path, winding steadily uphill for the first few minutes. It then levels out a bit to become more of a rocky, rooty, up-and-down, interesting trail, with lots of creeks and footbridges along the way. The trail is well used and very easy to follow, even without the yellow square markers on the trees.

About half an hour from the Lynn Peak junction you reach another signposted junction where the Lynn Loop Trail goes down to your left. The Headwaters Trail continues another 45 minutes or so north to its junction with the Cedars Mill Trail at the third debris chute, and beyond that to Norvan Falls (see hike #25), but you go downhill here on this short switchback connector path for about 10 minutes to where it meets the Cedars Mill Trail.

Go left at the bottom and follow this pleasant, wide, gradually sloping trail, with access to Lynn Creek on your right, for the next couple of kilometres. Watch for occasional remnants of logging activity, such as an old four-wheeled log transporter near the half-kilometre mark. In 20 to 25 minutes you reach the trailhead kiosk again, where you go right to cross the footbridge and return to the parking lot.

Walking through the "Enchanted Forest" on the way up Lynn Peak.

# 27 ▶ Lynn Creek and Rice Lake

> **Elevation gain:** 50 metres (165 feet)
> **High point:** 200 metres (650 feet)
> **Season:** Year-round
> **Topographical map:** North Vancouver 92G06
> **Hiking time:** 1½ to 2 hours
> Dogs not permitted on Rice Lake Loop Trail

This short, easy, year-round hike treats you to a very pleasant stroll alongside Lynn Creek and a visit to scenic, tranquil Rice Lake, which abounds with both fishing opportunities and a history of early 1900s' logging activities. You start in Lynn Headwaters Regional Park, going south along Lynn Creek, up to the man-made Rice Lake in the Lower Seymour Conservation Reserve (LSCR) and back to Lynn Headwaters.

From Highway 1 in North Vancouver, take Exit 19 to go north on Lynn Valley Road. After passing a shopping centre then the lights at Mountain Highway, watch for signs for Lynn Headwaters Park (passing the turnoff for Lynn Canyon Park) and park in the small paved lot at the end of the access road or in either of the two overflow lots. The park is administered by Metro Vancouver and was reopened to the public in 1985 after being closed since 1928 as part of the North Shore watershed system.

Begin on the Varley Trail at the entrance to the paved lot or down the stairs from either of the overflow lots. This trail, named after renowned Group of Seven artist and former Lynn Valley resident Frederick Varley, connects Lynn Headwaters with the LSCR. You head back southeast along this well-maintained trail, with its long boardwalks over marshy areas and Lynn Creek close by on your left. There is a short uphill stretch before you emerge onto a gravel road. At Rice Lake Road go left to take the large, sturdy footbridge across Lynn Creek, now deep in the canyon below.

Go straight ahead up a gentle slope for about 5 minutes to a large, grassy, open area with a pagoda, picnic tables, water fountain and toilets. This area, with its nearby parking lot at the top of Lillooet Road, is an excellent connecting point to several longer excursions: Lynn Canyon and the Baden-Powell Trail to the south (see hikes #19 and #20); the LSCR trail system to the east (see hikes #30 and #31); and the Upper Fisherman's Trail to the north (see hike #29).

Saving those for other days, you follow the signs to Rice Lake, about 500 metres (one-third mile) north. Stay on the trail to the

Looking across Rice Lake to Mount Seymour.

left as you pass the Learning Lodge, rather than going to the right on the paved Seymour Valley Trailway, and turn right at the signposted junction for Rice Lake a couple of minutes later (the beginning of the no-dogs area). Immediately to your left is a flume display and storyboard illustrating how in the early 1900s long wooden flumes were used to transport shingle bolts (long, wedge-shaped blocks of cedar from which shakes and shingles were cut) from Rice Lake down to Moodyville. That settlement, founded on Burrard Inlet in 1863, was named Moodyville in 1872 after sawmill owner Sewell Moody and was renamed the City of North Vancouver in 1907.

Continue along the wide Rice Lake Trail, turning right at the next junction to take the Loop Trail counter-clockwise around the lake. In about 50 metres (165 feet) you reach a lovely viewpoint looking north across the lake. Five minutes later you come to the Douglas Mowat Fisheries Project, which is dedicated to the memory of the former MLA, founder of the BC Paraplegic Association and champion of the rights of the disabled. This spot is an excellent lake lookout and a popular fishing area. The signposted junction has a short connector trail out to the Seymour

Valley Trailway, but you continue north on the Loop Trail around the lake, noticing the abundance of viewpoints and fishing spots along the way.

Just after passing a second connector trail to the Seymour Valley Trailway, you come to the lake outflow point and another storyboard. It describes the use of Rice Lake by the Hastings Shingle Manufacturing Company in the early 1900s to store cedar shingle bolts prior to their being transported on the flume line down to Moodyville. Next, the 400-metre (quarter-mile) unmarked Ecology Loop is worth a side trip, with a storyboard that provides some additional information on early 1900s' logging activity here. Back on the Loop Trail, a few minutes later you come to a signposted junction with a connector trail out to Lynn Headwaters, but unless you are in a hurry, stay to the left to continue around the lake.

In another few minutes a storyboard on your right describes how Rice Lake was converted by the City of North Vancouver in 1912 from a shingle bolt storage area to a drinking water reservoir, as backup to the Lynn Creek system. There is also a memorial here to the passengers and crew of Trans Canada Airlines flight 3, which crashed in 1947 on a remote area just west of Mount Elsay (visible to the north on a clear day) and was not found until 1994.

Now continue just down the hill to the next signposted junction to complete the circuit of this very pretty, serene little lake. You pass the flume display again before emerging at the connector trail. Here you turn right and follow this wide pathway northwest back into Lynn Headwaters Park.

About 10 minutes later you reach the Lynn Headwaters/LSCR Boundary signpost, where the Lynn Loop/Lynn Peak Trail heads up to the right. Lynn Peak and Lynn Loop would be a good hike for another day (see hike #26), but for now you continue straight ahead for another 5 minutes or so until you come to the Lynn Headwaters trailhead kiosk. Norvan Falls (see hike #25) and several more ambitious hikes (Hanes Valley, Lynn Lake, Coliseum Mountain) originate from here, but today you go left and across the footbridge back to the parking lot.

# 28 ▶ Richard Juryn Trail/ Old Lillooet Trail

> **Elevation gain:** 170 metres (550 feet)
> **High point:** 220 metres (720 feet)
> **Season:** Year-round
> **Topographical map:** North Vancouver 92G06
> **Hiking time:** 1¾ to 2¼ hours
> Dog-friendly

This all-season North Vancouver hike, with only moderate elevation gain, combines a loop around the scenic Richard Juryn Memorial Trail with a return trip on part of the historic Old Lillooet Trail south along Lynn Creek. It takes you from the trailhead at the top of Premier Street, around the Richard Juryn (RJ) Trail, then over to Lynn Canyon via the Baden-Powell (BP) Trail and back along Lynn Creek to the trailhead.

The Richard Juryn Trail is dedicated to the memory of Richard Juryn, who died October 7, 2007, in a tragic kayaking accident on Howe Sound. Richard was very involved in the community and had dreamed of building a trail network on the North Shore. His dream was realized with the construction of this trail through a massive effort by over 250 North Shore Mountain Bike Association and other volunteers on July 19, 2008.

From Highway 1 in North Vancouver, take Exit 22 (Lillooet

Road). Turn left at the light to drive north on Lillooet Road, then left at the next light onto Old Lillooet Road. Follow it around behind the Holiday Inn, then turn right onto Premier Street. Follow it north, going left at the Inter River Park sign, then right up a short hill to the RJ trailhead sign at the end of the parking lot.

Begin by following the path north and clockwise around the playing field, noticing Grouse Mountain (see hike #22), Mount Fromme (see hike #23) and Lynn Peak (see hike #26) off in the distance. Watch for the RJ sign that directs you out of the playing field area and up Inter River Park Road to Lillooet Road. Go left on Lillooet Road, passing the North Shore Equestrian Centre on your

Mount Seymour's Power Lines Trail from the Richard Juryn Trail lookout.

left. Just past Boal Chapel, stay left to follow the RJ signs up a short stretch of paved road through the North Vancouver Cemetery, rejoining Lillooet Road a few minutes later. Cross the road at the RJ signpost about 100 metres (330 feet) ahead and continue north.

In about 10 minutes you reach another RJ signpost where you turn right into the woods. About 50 metres (165 feet) in, you come to a bench and a viewpoint south toward Vancouver and Burnaby. From here you follow the wide, winding gravel path uphill under the power lines, reaching a small grassy area with another bench and a picnic table about 5 minutes later. Continue uphill and follow the RJ signs to its junction with the BP Trail (see hike #20) a few minutes later and half an hour or so from the start.

Pick up the RJ directly across the BP and follow it north into the forest. Three other trails branch off in the first few minutes, but you continue straight ahead, now with the sound of the Seymour River off to your right. About 10 minutes from the BP, follow the series of RJ signposts that lead you uphill and to the west. After a few more minutes there is another RJ signpost indicating a viewpoint to your left, about 45 minutes to an hour from the start. From the top of the bluff you look south and east to the lower slopes of Mount Seymour. Return to the signpost and continue along the trail, following it west and downhill until you emerge at its junction with the BP about 5 minutes from the lookout point.

You could continue south from here directly across the BP to retrace your steps on the RJ back to the start, but an alternative route that provides some additional variety is to take the BP west to Lynn Canyon, then follow Lynn Creek south back to the RJ trailhead.

Go right on the BP for a couple of minutes before arriving at Lillooet Road. The BP, well marked with orange "BP" fleur-de-lis triangles on the trees, continues into the forest at the signpost across the road. Soon you hear Lynn Creek off in the distance, and in another few minutes you arrive at a signposted junction with the Old Lillooet Trail, named after an ill-fated old cattle trail built in the 1870s from Lillooet to Moodyville on the north shore of Burrard Inlet.

Here the BP continues downhill to the right, but you go left and south along this well-maintained trail. Soon you start your descent into Lynn Canyon. The trail is rather rocky and rooty in places, but does have some boardwalks across the marshy areas. In 15 to 20 minutes from the last BP junction you have Lynn Creek close by on your right.

Before long the forest opens up and the trail levels out into a wide dirt path. Stay to the right, and in about another 10 minutes you come to a trail junction, with a footbridge across Lynn Creek on your right and a trail heading uphill to your left. Take the latter, checking the abundant nearby bushes for ripe blackberries during August. At the top of the hill go right as the trail leads you back past the Inter River Park playing field and to the parking lot in another 5 minutes.

# 29 ▶ Upper Fisherman's Trail

**Elevation gain:** 140 metres (460 feet)
**High point:** 250 metres (820 feet)
**Season:** Most of the year
**Topographical map:** North Vancouver 92G06
**Hiking time:** 3½ to 4 hours, including lunch
Dogs not permitted on Upper Fisherman's Trail

This scenic trail, significantly upgraded in 2013, combines minimal elevation gain with magnificent mountain vistas as you make your way north along the banks of the Seymour River. The Seymour Valley was an off-limits watershed from 1928 to 1987, when it was reopened to the public as part of the Seymour Demonstration Forest, later renamed the Lower Seymour Conservation Reserve (LSCR) and administered by Metro Vancouver. The 12- to 14-kilometre (7½- to 9-mile) round trip takes you from the trailhead at the top of Lillooet Road in North Vancouver, down the Homestead Trail and along the Fisherman's Trail to the Spur 4 Bridge and Mid-Valley Viewpoint, then back to your starting point by either of two return routes.

From Highway 1 in North Vancouver, take Exit 22 (Lillooet Road). Turn left at the light to drive north on Lillooet Road. Continue until you come to the gravel parking lot next to the Seymour-Capilano Filtration Plant, the largest water filtration

plant in Canada. This is not a pay lot, but watch for the signs telling you when the gates are locked for the night. Nearby there is an Info Centre and Parks office, as well as a grassy, open area with a pagoda, picnic tables, water fountain and toilets.

You begin by going east on the footpath along the top of the parking lot and past the entrance to the water filtration plant area to a signposted junction for the two trails that lead down into the LSCR. Leaving the Twin Bridges Trail for another day, stay to the left and descend on the very pleasant Homestead Trail for about 15 minutes or so, passing through an enchanted forest of moss-covered maple and alder and noticing the growing sound of the Seymour River off in the distance.

Turn left at the intersection with the Fisherman's Trail (the beginning of the no-dogs area). Follow this wide, well-travelled trail, part of which is quite a long boardwalk over some wet areas, as it winds its way north along the banks of the Seymour River. Occasionally you see remnants of the logging days of the early 1900s in the form of large, old-growth stumps, many of which have since become nurse logs for newer-generation trees. After an hour or so of minimal elevation gain you reach a wide gravel road

Runner Peak and Mount Elsay from the Mid-Valley Viewpoint picnic area.

that has occasional vehicle traffic going across the Spur 4 Bridge and beyond.

A short side trip down the road will take you to the bridge itself, but to get to the Mid-Valley Viewpoint take the trail into the woods directly across the road. In about 5 minutes you arrive at your destination, a nice grassy area with toilets, picnic tables and a covered picnic area. Enjoy the views of Mount Seymour, Runner Peak and Mount Elsay across the valley to the east as you eat your lunch. You may be visited by the occasional raven looking for food scraps.

Now refreshed by your picnic lunch, follow the signs for the Seymour Valley Trailway via the Hydraulic Connector Trail (named after nearby Hydraulic Creek). This 400-metre (quarter-mile) trail leads west into the woods and crosses the Seymour Mainline Road, which is closed to the public. After a couple of minutes you see a signpost indicating the Butterfly Garden off to the right. A nearby storyboard explains how the area, once used as a bomb disposal site by the RCMP, has been transformed into a habitat for some twenty species of butterflies. Leaving the Butterfly Garden and continuing up the Connector Trail, you pass through another amazing enchanted forest where it seems as if almost every tree branch is draped with moss, a testimony to the area's heavy annual rainfall.

At this point you have two possibilities for your return trip to the Lillooet Road parking lot, with roughly equal return times. You can turn around here and return to the Mid-Valley Viewpoint, then retrace your steps back along the Fisherman's Trail and up the Homestead Trail to the parking lot.

Alternatively, you can continue up the Connector Trail to reach the Seymour Valley Trailway junction, where you go left. While this 6-kilometre (4-mile) stretch of undulating paved road is rather uninspiring, it does have a couple of points of interest. After 25 to 30 minutes or so, you reach the Balloon Picnic Area (at Balloon Creek). A storyboard a few minutes ahead describes how in 1967 there was some experimental balloon logging salvage activity in this area. After about another half hour, you reach the Rice Creek Picnic Area. On the right-hand side of the road is a connector trail leading to the nearby Rice Lake Loop Trail. This trail could be an alternative way back if you have an extra hour or so to circle scenic Rice Lake (see hike #27 for guidance), then follow the signs from Rice Lake back to the Lillooet Road parking lot.

A little farther along the Trailway there is another Rice Lake connector trail, this one leading to the Douglas Mowat fishing wharf. A few metres ahead a storyboard marks the site of the original Rice Lake Road, circa 1910. It also gives some insight into homesteader S. Smith's use of this area as a pasture or corral for livestock until the 1930s. Continuing along the Trailway, you reach the parking lot area in another few minutes.

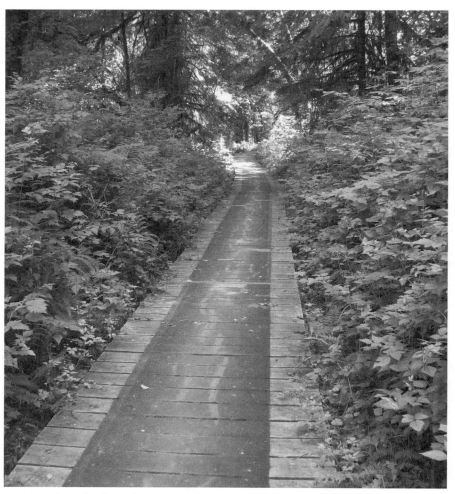

A long boardwalk on the Upper Fisherman's Trail.

lines and straight ahead for another few minutes, past the sign-posted Richard Juryn Trail junctions (see hike #28), before arriving at Lillooet Road. The BP continues into the forest at a signpost immediately across the road. Soon you hear Lynn Creek off in the distance, and in about 10 minutes you arrive at a signposted junction with the Old Lillooet Trail to Premier Street. Here you go down to the right to descend into Lynn Canyon. Partway along the boardwalk across a marshy area, you see a small beach at the side of Lynn Creek. The beach is a good spot for a water stop and a rest at the water's edge.

Continue up Lynn Canyon for 10 to 15 minutes before you come to Twin Falls Bridge. In the summer months you may see cliff jumpers here. Don't cross the bridge, but continue up the east side of the canyon for another 10 to 15 minutes before coming to a sign for the suspension bridge on your left. A short detour across the suspension bridge will take you to the Lynn Canyon Ecology Centre and the Lynn Canyon Café building, with a concession and washrooms.

The BP continues across the suspension bridge, but you stay on the east side of Lynn Canyon all the way up. Once the trail levels out it becomes a wide, winding gravel path. Stay left at the Seymour-Capilano Filtration Plant to continue going north. About

A small Lynn Creek beach just off the Baden-Powell trail.

15 minutes from the suspension bridge you reach a grassy, open area with a pagoda, picnic tables, water fountain and toilets. This area is roughly the halfway point of the hike and another good spot for a rest. If time permits, a one-hour side trip might be the signposted trail to Rice Lake, about 500 metres (one-third mile) north (see hike #27).

From the pagoda you go east toward the Info Centre and Parks office, then along the top of a gravel parking lot and past the water filtration plant area to a signposted junction for the two trails that lead down into the Lower Seymour Conservation Reserve. Leaving the Homestead Trail for another day, turn right and descend on the wide, gravel Twin Bridges Trail. About 25 minutes later you reach the Twin Bridges/Fisherman's Trail junction. Only one of the original two bridges remains (rebuilt in 2009); cross it and continue south along the east bank of the Seymour River. A small sandy beach just below the bridge on the east side (when the river is low enough) can be reached by a set of steps on your right.

There are three possibilities from here to return to Hyannis. The first and longest is the signposted junction with the Mystery Creek Trail about 5 minutes from the twin bridge. It is a fairly steep trail and you need to be alert for mountain bikers who may be descending. After about 10 minutes of uphill plodding you reach the Power Lines Trail, where you turn right and continue uphill for another few minutes to the Mystery Creek footbridge. Turning right immediately after the footbridge will take you back to the Hyannis Connector and out to Hyannis in 15 to 20 minutes.

Alternatively, you can continue along the Fisherman's Trail for another few minutes after the Mystery Creek junction and turn up the signposted Bridle Path Trail. This is a shorter, easier ascent than Mystery Creek. At the top, after 12 to 15 minutes of climbing, you go right and along a winding boardwalk, then right again at a T-junction with the Hyannis Connector out to Hyannis.

The third option is to continue along the Fisherman's Trail from the Bridle Path junction, enjoying more of the Seymour River canyon. In 10 to 15 minutes you reach its junction with the BP from Hyannis, just before the Riverside Drive trailhead. Here you go left and retrace your steps back up to Hyannis where you started.

# 31 ▶ Lower Seymour Conservation Reserve

> **Elevation gain:** 130 metres (420 feet)
> **High point:** 200 metres (650 feet)
> **Season:** Year-round
> **Topographical map:** North Vancouver 92G06
> **Hiking time:** 2½ to 3 hours
> Dog-friendly

The Lower Seymour Conservation Reserve (LSCR), administered by Metro Vancouver, was once known as the Seymour Demonstration Forest. Part of the 18,000-hectare (44,460-acre) Seymour Watershed from 1928 to 1987, this 5,668-hectare (14,000-acre) forest was reopened to the public and now offers diverse hiking opportunities through a landscape of forested slopes and spectacular river views. This circuit includes sites of early 1900s' homesteading activities, as well as an LSCR fisheries enhancement project. For your workout, there is also some elevation gain on both sides of the Seymour River. Starting from the trailhead at Hyannis Drive in North Vancouver, you go down to the Seymour River, around a Twin Bridges–Homestead Trail loop on its west side, then back along the river and up to Hyannis.

From Highway 1 in North Vancouver, take Exit 22 (Mount Seymour Parkway). Going east on Mount Seymour Parkway, turn left at Berkley Road. At the top of Berkley turn left onto Hyannis Drive and park anywhere in that one-block section of Hyannis.

Begin by taking the Hyannis Connector at the west end of Hyannis. Follow this trail for 8 to 10 minutes to the first of two junctions with the Bridle Path Trail, where you turn left and start along a winding boardwalk. Just after the end of the boardwalk you see on your left a GVRD signpost that marks the continuation of the Bridle Path down to the Seymour River. After about 10

A moss-covered arch from an early 1900s' Seymour River homestead.

minutes of gentle downhill on this fine gravel path, you come to a signposted junction with the Fisherman's Trail.

Turn right here, and continue along the Fisherman's Trail for a few minutes until you reach the Twin Bridges, of which only one remains. A nearby Metro Vancouver storyboard explains that the first bridge (the lower one, carrying a water main and providing pedestrian east-west access) was built in 1907–08 and dismantled in 1992. A second bridge was built in 1926 and eventually replaced by the present "blue bridge" in 2009. Cross this bridge and continue straight ahead up the wide, gravel Twin Bridges Trail. In 25 to 35 minutes you reach its junction on your right with the Homestead Trail, near the Seymour-Capilano Filtration Plant. A short detour west past the water filtration plant area and across the top of the gravel parking lot will take you to a grassy, open area with a pagoda, picnic tables, water fountain and toilets. You next take the very pleasant Homestead Trail for 15 minutes or so downhill to its intersection with the Fisherman's Trail.

Going left here would take you north along the Upper Fisherman's Trail to the Mid-Valley Viewpoint (see hike #29), but for today go right to follow the Fisherman's Trail south, and watch for signs on your left of the early 1900s' homestead activity in this area. The first, after about 100 metres (330 feet), is a small, moss-covered gate, through which an old narrow trail leads about 25 metres (80 feet) to a long-abandoned concrete foundation on your left next to the river. A little farther along the main trail are the larger, moss-covered arches of another homestead, part of the small settlement along the river's edge before the Seymour Valley was designated a protected watershed in the 1920s. If you look closely on either side of the arches you will see that several mossy old fence posts, with little round holes for the fence rails, are still standing.

About 200 metres (650 feet) farther along on your right is the Homestead Fisheries Enhancement Area. Some storyboards along a small side trail explain how the new creeks and pools were constructed to provide additional salmonid spawning habitat in the lower Seymour River.

Strolling along for another 5 minutes you reach an obvious but unmarked side trail on your left. About 15 metres (50 feet) in, partially obscured by brush, there is quite a large, old, brick and concrete fireplace just off the trail on your left-hand side, another remnant of the homesteading cabins from the early 1900s.

A couple of minutes more along the Fisherman's Trail you see a tunnel cut into the rock face on your right. A storyboard explains that the tunnel, completed in 1907, was once used for a wooden water pipeline. It also describes how the nearby pool in the Seymour River was once used to store shingle bolts (long, wedge-shaped blocks of cedar from which shakes and shingles were cut) for the Hastings Shingle Manufacturing Company. On your left just past the tunnel entrance stands one lone telephone pole from those early homesteading days.

Continuing along the Fisherman's Trail for another few minutes you once again reach the signposted junction with the Twin Bridges Trail. Cross the bridge and continue south along the east bank of the Seymour River. Note that a small, sandy beach just below the bridge on the east side (when the river is low enough) can be reached by a set of steps on your right.

There are two possibilities from here to return to Hyannis. The first and longer one is the signposted junction with the Mystery Creek trail about 5 minutes from the twin bridge. It is a fairly steep trail and you need to be alert for mountain bikers who may be descending. After about 10 minutes of uphill plodding you reach the Power Lines Trail, where you turn right and continue uphill for another few minutes to the Mystery Creek footbridge. Turning right immediately after the footbridge will take you back to the Hyannis Connector and out to Hyannis in 15 to 20 minutes.

Alternatively you can continue along the Fisherman's Trail for another few minutes after the Mystery Creek junction and go back up the Bridle Path Trail on which you descended from Hyannis.

The Hyannis Connector Trail in late February.

# 32 ▶ Mushroom Parking Lot

> **Elevation gain:** 350 metres (1,150 feet)
> **High point:** 500 metres (1,650 feet)
> **Season:** April to November
> **Topographical map:** Port Coquitlam 92G07
> **Hiking time:** 2½ to 4 hours
> Dog-friendly

A visit to the Mushroom Parking Lot provides an opportunity to experience some of Mount Seymour's fascinating history from the early 1900s. You can combine this introduction to one of the more strenuous sections of the Baden-Powell (BP) Trail with other return options to experience a scenic, energetic and varied round trip. The hike takes you from the trailhead at Hyannis Drive in North Vancouver up the BP Trail to the historic Mushroom Parking Lot, with three options for your return route.

From Highway 1 in North Vancouver, take Exit 22 (Mount Seymour Parkway). Going east on Mount Seymour Parkway, turn left at Berkley Road. At the top of Berkley turn left onto Hyannis Drive and park anywhere in that one-block section of Hyannis.

Begin by taking the signposted BP Trail on the north side of Hyannis. The trail is well marked with orange "BP" fleur-de-lis triangles on the trees. There are lots of roots and rocks on this trail, so watch your footing, particularly if it's wet. Follow the BP alongside Canyon Creek, going steadily uphill until you meet the Bridle Path Trail at a footbridge 15 to 20 minutes from Hyannis. Go to the right here, on the joint BP/Bridle Path Trail. At the next signposted T-junction where the trails part, about 70 metres (230 feet) ahead, you turn left to follow the BP north. The Bridle Path, one of your possible return routes, continues in a roughly south-easterly direction across the lower slopes of Mount Seymour (see hike #34).

Soon you leave the stream behind and the BP starts a fairly steep climb, possibly reminding you of tackling the Grouse Grind.

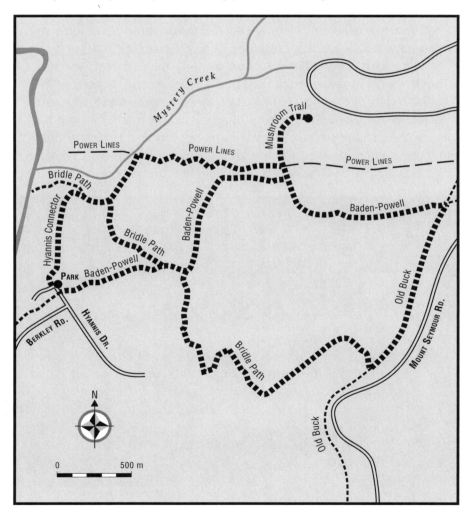

After about a half hour or more of steady uphill plodding, the trail levels out a bit near its signposted intersection with the top of Severed D (a.k.a. Good Samaritan), a good place for a water stop.

Continuing east along the BP for 5 minutes or so you reach a signposted junction with the Mushroom Trail. Turn left here and you are now headed north toward the Mushroom Parking Lot. After about another 5 minutes you reach a signposted junction with the Power Lines Trail. Continue straight ahead into the woods on the Mushroom Trail, which now begins to look more like an old logging road as it heads gradually up through the eerily quiet forest. After 5 to 10 minutes watch for a sign to the right directing you to the Mushroom Parking Lot. Another couple of minutes and you have reached your destination, 1 to 1½ hours from the start.

The Mushroom Parking Lot itself is now overgrown with bushes and alder, but the original cedar stump, known as the Mushroom for the rounded roof that once protected it, still stands, partially enclosed by a rickety picket fence. A nearby storyboard outlines the site's history. It explains how in the 1920s the Buck Logging Road allowed vehicle traffic up to this point. A parking lot was cleared and travellers were able to leave their vehicles and

Late April snow at the site of the Mushroom Parking Lot.

continue up the mountain on foot. The Mushroom itself played an important role as an information board where announcements were posted for special events. However in the 1950s a new road was built to the top of Mount Seymour and the Mushroom's usefulness was ended. Along with the storyboard there are a couple of old photographs, one that shows the stump with its original mushroom-shaped cap and its notice board, and another that shows a number of early 1900s' autos in the parking lot.

To return, you can retrace your steps the same way you came up, but there are two other options. Leaving the Mushroom and arriving at the Power Lines again, you can turn right down the fairly steep and rocky Power Lines Trail. On your way down you are treated to views of West Vancouver and beyond. Soon you hear Mystery Creek off to your right and shortly afterwards you see the Mystery Creek footbridge, 20 to 30 minutes from the Power Lines/Mushroom junction. Turn left just before the footbridge and follow the Hyannis Connector, staying on that main wide trail for about 15 minutes all the way out to Hyannis.

A longer alternative is to follow the original route used by the vehicle traffic, continuing down the Mushroom Trail to its junction with the BP. Here you stay left, following the BP east for 15 to 20 minutes to where it meets the Old Buck Trail, once the logging road used by the Buck's Logging Company in the 1920s. Go right and downhill on Old Buck, then after another 15 to 20 minutes go right again on the Bridle Path. You are now going west on the Bridle Path, following its red square markers on the trees.

After another 40 to 60 minutes turn left at its intersection with the BP and left again in about 70 metres (230 feet), just before the footbridge over Canyon Creek, to return to Hyannis in a total time of 1½ to 2 hours from the BP/Mushroom junction. Another option that adds about another 15 minutes is to continue across the footbridge and along the Bridle Path to the signposted T-junction where it meets the Hyannis Connector, and turn left there to return to Hyannis.

# 33 ▸ The TNT Trail

**Elevation gain:** 370 metres (1,200 feet)
**High point:** 520 metres (1,700 feet)
**Season:** April to November
**Hiking time:** 2½ to 3½ hours
**Topographical map:** Port Coquitlam 92G07
Dog-friendly

On this "trail less travelled" you venture up one of Mount Seymour's lesser-known but quite interesting hiking trails, with the option of taking a few minutes to visit the historic Mushroom Parking Lot on the way back. Starting from the trailhead at Hyannis Drive in North Vancouver you head up the TNT trail, connect to the old Cabin Trail and then complete the loop by returning to Hyannis on the rugged Baden-Powell (BP) Trail. Be aware that the TNT route is somewhat remote and not well marked, so exercise caution when following these trails.

From Highway 1 in North Vancouver, take Exit 22 (Mount Seymour Parkway). Going east on Mount Seymour Parkway, turn left at Berkley Road. At the top of Berkley turn left onto Hyannis Drive and park anywhere in that one-block section of Hyannis.

You begin by taking the Hyannis Connector at the west end of Hyannis. Follow this trail north, passing a signposted junction with the Bridle Path on your right in 10 to 15 minutes and coming to the Power Lines Trail about 5 minutes later. Here you go left and across the Mystery Creek footbridge. At the top of the short hill you turn right, taking that trail into the forest. Follow it for about 5 minutes to a signposted junction with the Greenland, TNT and NEDS trails.

Between Greenland and the NEDS ramps, cross over the first of several large fallen trees to start up the TNT, whose name can be attributed to an old dynamite shack found in the area. Follow the well-worn TNT roughly northeast as it gains elevation. Watch for

An old corduroy logging road on the TNT trail.

occasional faded red "T" flags on the trees. The trail is steep and rocky at first, then has long stretches of old corduroy logging road, so watch your footing if it's wet.

After 35 to 45 minutes on TNT you reach its junction with Lumpy Gravy on your right. This junction is no longer marked; Lumpy Gravy has not been maintained and should not be attempted unless you have travelled it before and know it well. Continue up the TNT trail, enjoying its relative seclusion and following it northeast until it loops around to meet the top of the Cabin Trail (marked by a "CBN00" sign on a tree), at which point you follow the Cabin Trail south and gradually downhill.

A few minutes after passing its T-junction with Dirty Diapers on your right you reach a branch of Mystery Creek with a small waterfall (take care if spring runoff levels are high). After another 5 minutes or so you come to a signpost directing you to the left for the Mushroom Parking Lot, a quick side trip if you have an extra few minutes. The Mushroom is now overgrown with bushes and alder, but the original cedar stump still stands, partially enclosed by a rickety picket fence, and a storyboard and photographs outline the site's history from the 1920s (see hike #32).

To continue your descent, follow either signposted trail south and downhill from the Mushroom. After about 10 minutes you reach the Power Lines Trail. Continue straight ahead for another couple of minutes until you come to the BP. Turn right and follow the BP west, passing its signposted junction with the top of Severed D (a.k.a. Good Samaritan) in about 5 minutes. You soon start down a fairly steep section of the BP as it heads west and then south toward Hyannis.

In a half hour or so from Severed D, you reach the BP's signposted junction with the Bridle Path. Go right here on the joint BP/Bridle Path Trail for about 70 metres (230 feet), until you come to the next junction just before a footbridge, where the trails part. Here you go left on the BP, following it alongside Canyon Creek for another 15 to 20 minutes out to Hyannis.

# 34 ▶ Bridle Path Ramble

**Elevation gain:** 100 metres (330 feet)
**High point:** 250 metres (820 feet)
**Season:** Year-round
**Topographical map:** Port Coquitlam 92G07
**Hiking time:** 1¼ to 1¾ hours
Dog-friendly

Here is a short, easy, delightful all-weather ramble on the wooded slopes of lower Mount Seymour. This charming trail accommodates hikers of all ages, with several crossings of picturesque little creeks on well-engineered wooden footbridges, and a variety of trail surfaces. The hike takes you from the trailhead at Hyannis Drive in North Vancouver east along the lower slopes of Mount Seymour via the Bridle Path Trail, with a loop back to Hyannis along the Northlands Golf Course and Blair Range trails.

From Highway 1 in North Vancouver, take Exit 22 (Mount Seymour Parkway). Going east on Mount Seymour Parkway, turn left at Berkley Road. At the top of Berkley turn left onto Hyannis Drive and park anywhere in that one-block section of Hyannis.

Begin by taking the Hyannis Connector at the west end of Hyannis. Follow it north for 10 to 15 minutes to a signposted junction with the Bridle Path Trail, where you turn right, go up a short hill and then along a winding boardwalk. The subject of much trail improvement work over the last few years, including 2013, the Bridle Path traverses the lower slopes of Mount Seymour in a roughly southeasterly direction, with lots of ups and downs along the way, but minimal elevation gain.

After 15 to 20 minutes from the Hyannis Connector junction you come to Canyon Creek, the first of several creeks and footbridges you will encounter. Just across the bridge there is a signposted junction with the Baden-Powell (BP) Trail. You continue straight ahead on the joint BP/Bridle Path Trail, while at the next signposted T-junction where the trails part, about 70 metres (230 feet) ahead, you turn right on the Bridle Path while the BP heads left and north toward the Mushroom Parking Lot (see hike #32) and Deep Cove (see hike #20).

You pass various other trail intersections along the way, but in general keep watching for the Bridle Path signs on the trees. Just under 10 minutes from the BP junction, you come to a signposted

Some recent trail work on the Bridle Path.

fork in the trail, with a small metal "Bridle Path" plaque on the tree in the centre. The Bridle Path continues downhill to the right, but you may choose to go left on the aptly named Cardiac Bypass, saving yourself a few minutes and a little elevation gain. The Cardiac Bypass rejoins the Bridle Path just before the next footbridge at McCartney Creek.

About 25 to 30 minutes from the BP junction you notice the Northlands Golf Course through the trees on your right and see a chain-link fence ahead. Just before the fence there is an unmarked junction with the Golf Course Trail, where you go downhill and to the right. Follow that trail to head back west along the northern edge of the golf course for about 5 minutes (watch for errant golf balls) until you reach a large boulder outcropping on your right. Take this trail back into the woods, staying to the left at the first junction and right at the next two, to go roughly northwest for a couple of minutes.

The woods start to open up now, changing from mostly evergreen to mostly deciduous trees. This opening marks the beginning of the Blair Range area, now overgrown with salmonberry bushes and alder but used for many years as a military rifle and machine gun practice range. As you curve to the west along the flat Blair Range Trail, you cross the first of three small streams, which may require using a fallen log as a handhold, depending on water runoff levels.

Other smaller trails branch off, but keep going straight ahead and west on the main wide trail. In a few more minutes you see an opening in the trees ahead of you. Here the trail emerges onto a back lane just beyond a chain-link fence and gate. This lane can be a good source of blackberries during August, but you turn right here for a short uphill path that in a couple of minutes takes you onto the east end of Hyannis. Walk along Hyannis for not quite 10 minutes back to where you left your vehicle at its western end.

# 35 ► Mount Seymour Vancouver Picnic Area

> **Elevation gain:** 430 metres (1,400 feet)
> **High point:** 550 metres (1,800 feet)
> **Season:** April to November
> **Topographical map:** Port Coquitlam 92G07
> **Hiking time:** 2½ to 3½ hours
> Dog-friendly

After a fairly long slog up the forested lower slopes of Mount Seymour, you can relax at a grassy picnic area, then choose from a couple of options for your return trip, including a stop at the historic Mushroom Parking Lot. This hike takes you from the Old Buck trailhead in North Vancouver to the Vancouver Picnic Area on Mount Seymour, then back via your choice of return routes.

From Highway 1 in North Vancouver, take Exit 22 (Mount Seymour Parkway). Going east on Mount Seymour Parkway, turn left at Mount Seymour Road. Just after passing Indian River Drive on the right, you turn left onto Anne Macdonald Way and park either in or close to the Old Buck trailhead parking lot.

Starting up the Old Buck Trail, you see a signposted junction after about 130 metres (425 feet), but continue straight ahead on what was once a logging road used by the Buck's Logging Company in the 1920s. After 10 to 15 minutes you reach its signposted junction with the Bridle Path, but continue uphill for another 15 to 25 minutes, when you pass a signposted junction with the Baden-Powell (BP) Trail on your left. This is where you come out later if you take a side trip on your way back. About 80 metres (260 feet) ahead, you see the BP branching off to the right to head east toward Deep Cove (see hike #20), but you continue uphill on Old Buck. Soon you cross the Power Lines Trail and in another 10 minutes or so you reach a yellow gate at Mount Seymour Road.

Pick up Old Buck again a few metres downhill across the road. Continue uphill for a few more minutes, when you reach the

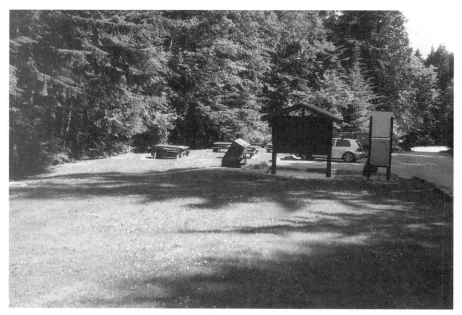

Mount Seymour Vancouver Picnic Area.

signposted junction for the Old Buck Access Trail. Turn left here, leaving the Upper Old Buck and Perimeter trails up to Mount Seymour's lake area for another day (see hike #38). The Access Trail is a more pleasing, gradual ascent than Old Buck has been so far. Follow it west for 20 to 30 minutes, watching for the orange flashing on the trees, until you emerge at the Vancouver Picnic Area, after about 1¼ to 1¾ hours of continuous uphill from the Old Buck trailhead. There is a grassy area with picnic tables, and toilets across the road. This spot, originally known as Vancouver Lookout until the growing trees eventually obscured the view, is often used as a drop-off point for mountain bikers headed downhill.

After a well-earned break you are ready for the return trip. You can retrace your steps the same way you came up, but there are other possibilities for the way back. Follow the paved road from the picnic area a few metres downhill to Mount Seymour Road. Across the road and about 120 metres (390 feet) uphill there is a signpost where the trail enters the woods. There you see a large Seymour Trails map, which may help you get your bearings on where you are and decide between two choices for the return trip.

If time permits, you can make a side trip to the historic Mushroom Parking Lot. Follow the fittingly named Incline Trail downhill for about 5 minutes, turn right at the signposted junction with the Mushroom Trail and continue for another few minutes until you reach the Mushroom itself. The site is now overgrown with bushes and alder, but the original cedar stump still stands, partially enclosed by a rickety picket fence, and a storyboard and photographs outline the site's history from the 1920s (see hike #32).

To continue your descent from the Mushroom, follow the signposted trail downhill toward the BP/Mushroom junction. In a few minutes you reach the Power Lines Trail. Continue straight ahead into the woods for another 5 minutes or so until you reach the BP. Here you stay left and follow the orange "BP" fleur-de-lis triangles on the trees east for 15 to 20 minutes to the signposted junction where the BP meets Old Buck. Go right on Old Buck and follow it all the way downhill to the parking lot.

A rougher but more direct route back from the Seymour Trails map is to continue downhill on the Incline Trail, listening for bikers who may be coming up quickly behind you. After about 10 minutes you reach the Power Lines Trail again. Go left here for about 25 metres (80 feet), then right to continue down the unmarked Incline Trail for about another 10 minutes, when you reach its unmarked T-junction with the BP. Go left on the BP, following the orange "BP" fleur-de-lis triangles on the trees for 10 to 15 minutes or so until you reach its signposted junction with Old Buck. Here you turn right and follow Old Buck for another 20 to 30 minutes downhill to the parking lot.

# 36 ▶ Dinkey Peak and Dog Mountain

> **Elevation gain:** 100 metres (330 feet)
> **High point:** 1,117 metres (3,665 feet)
> **Season:** July to October
> **Topographical map:** Port Coquitlam 92G07
> **Hiking time:** 2½ to 3 hours
> Dog-friendly

This relatively straightforward North Vancouver hike requires minimal climbing, yet treats you to two quite accessible and impressive viewpoints with a pretty little subalpine lake thrown in for good measure. You trek from the Mount Seymour upper parking lot to nearby Dinkey Peak, then past First Lake and over to Dog Mountain before looping back. It is best done in midsummer to early fall, long after the snow melts and before the fall rains start, as these trails can be muddy and slippery in places at the best of times. In late summer Mount Seymour's ripe blueberries are an additional attraction to consider when planning your hike.

From Highway 1 in North Vancouver, take Exit 22 (Mount Seymour Parkway). Going east on Mount Seymour Parkway, turn left at Mount Seymour Road and proceed about 12 kilometres (7½ miles) up to the main parking area. There is a BC Parks information kiosk at the northwest corner of the parking lot, with a map and brief descriptions of the local trails.

Begin by heading north from the trailhead kiosk on the main trail toward the peaks of Mount Seymour. In about 100 metres (330 feet) a signposted trail branches off on your left; this is the more direct approach to Dog Mountain (about 2½ kilometres or 1½ miles) and is your route out on the way back. Continue uphill, staying left on the fairly steep, narrow, rocky trail rather than following the wide, gravel road on the right. In another few minutes you reach a signposted junction where the trail to Mount Seymour's three peaks continues straight ahead, but you go left on the 350-metre (quarter-mile) trail to Dinkey Peak.

About 5 minutes later you climb a short flight of stairs to emerge at a Dinkey Peak viewpoint. Although not the summit, this destination has fine views south, east and west over the Metro Vancouver area. To reach the Dinkey Peak summit, only a few metres higher at 1,117 metres (3,665 feet), go back down the stairs and follow the trail to the left for another 5 minutes or so before

Passing First Lake on the way to Dog Mountain.

climbing to the top of the large rocky bluff with its more expansive views, including north to the peaks of Mount Seymour and west to Crown Mountain.

To continue toward First Lake, follow the yellow BC Parks markers on the trees as they lead you downhill from the summit and back north again to a signposted junction about 10 minutes later. Go left here for First Lake and Dog Mountain along the rather rocky, rooty and often muddy trail.

In 10 to 15 minutes you emerge at charming First Lake in its picturesque subalpine meadow setting. The trail circles the lake, but since you go past the other side on the way back, stay right at the signposted junction to continue west around the lake toward Dog Mountain. Again following the somewhat rough, slippery trail with lots of roots and rocks, you reach Dog Mountain about 20 to 30 minutes from First Lake, and roughly 1½ hours from the parking lot.

Dog Mountain, at 1,050 metres (3,445 feet), offers panoramic views of the entire Lower Mainland, Fraser River delta and Point Roberts to the south, and Lynn Peak (see hike #26), Grouse

Mountain (see hike #22), Crown Mountain and Coliseum Mountain off to the west and northwest. Ravens and whisky jacks may be in nearby trees waiting for lunch leftovers.

When you are ready to return, retrace your steps to First Lake, where you stay to the right to take the shorter route back. At a steady pace you reach the parking lot in another 20 to 30 minutes, or a total of about 45 minutes to an hour from Dog Mountain.

Dog Mountain is also a popular winter hiking destination. Starting from the trailhead kiosk, take the shorter, more direct route to Dog Mountain and allow about an hour each way. You will need either snowshoes or hiking boots with crampons. The trail is well marked and easy to follow. In some ways (without all of the roots, rocks and mud) it is a smoother and more pleasant trek than the summertime one.

Looking southwest toward Metro Vancouver from Dog Mountain.

# 37 ▸ Mystery Lake and Mystery Peak

**Elevation gain:** 203 metres (665 feet)
**High point:** 1,220 metres (4,000 feet)
**Season:** July to October
**Topographical map:** Port Coquitlam 92G07
**Hiking time:** 1½ to 2 hours
Dog-friendly

Here is another fairly short but pleasant outing into Mount Seymour's subalpine area, with an inviting, peaceful little lake and a panoramic viewpoint to boot. Starting from the Mount Seymour upper parking lot, you first visit Mystery Lake, then continue north to make your way up Mystery Peak before returning via a circular route to the parking lot. This hike is best done in midsummer to early fall, long after the snow melts and before the fall rains start, as these trails can be muddy and slippery in places.

From Highway 1 in North Vancouver, take Exit 22 (Mount Seymour Parkway). Going east on Mount Seymour Parkway, turn left at Mount Seymour Road and proceed about 12 kilometres (7½ miles) up to the main parking area. There is a BC Parks information kiosk at the northwest corner of the parking lot, with a map and brief descriptions of the local trails.

Going north along the gravel road from the trailhead kiosk

for about 100 metres (330 feet), you reach a signposted junction at the Dog Mountain trailhead. Either the gravel road straight ahead or the Mount Seymour Main Trail to your left will be your return route. For now you turn right to go east from the signpost, which indicates a distance of 1.2 kilometres (.75 miles) to Mystery Lake. Passing under the Mystery Peak Chairlift and through an area of plentiful blueberry bushes, you follow the winding, somewhat rocky, rooty trail gradually uphill, with the chairlift on your left-hand side. This is an easy to follow, well-worn trail with red markers on the trees.

In 15 minutes or so, you reach tiny Nancy Lake on your right. Here a boardwalk covers a little muddy section where the trail skirts around the west side of the lake. A few minutes later you cross the Unicorn ski run, with its fine views off to the south as it curves down toward the Goldie and Flower lakes area (see hike #38). From here the trail gets a little steeper as you advance upwards toward Mystery Lake. You emerge onto its open, rocky, subalpine setting about 25 to 30 minutes from the start. There are numerous spots around the lake to sit and eat a lunch, have a quick swim or simply rest for a while.

When you are ready to leave Mystery Lake's scenic, peaceful setting, continue north on the same trail, skirting around the side of Mystery Peak and rising gradually until you reach the foot of the Brockton Point Chairlift in 10 minutes or so. Proceed about 100 metres (330 feet) west from here along the gravel road, then go left to take a wide, curving, rocky trail, which soon becomes a

Enjoying the summer sun at Mystery Lake near Mount Seymour.

narrow path, up the north side of Mystery Peak to its summit in about another 10 minutes from the chairlift.

From here you are treated to views south beyond the main parking area toward the Lower Mainland, as well as the nearby peaks of Dog Mountain and Mount Seymour's Pump (First) Peak. Take some time to enjoy the panoramic vistas in all directions before heading back, this time by following the green-signed, wide, rocky, Manning ski run as it curves downhill and to the west. In 5 to 10 minutes from the summit you reach a signposted junction offering two options for your return. The more direct route, with an approximate return time of 15 minutes, is to continue south down the Manning ski run, which becomes a wide gravel road as it nears the parking lot.

Alternatively you can go right here, dropping down to a small valley, to follow the main Mount Seymour Trail, a slightly longer but more interesting return option of about 1.2 kilometres (.75 miles) and 25 minutes or so to reach the parking lot. As you descend on this fairly steep, rocky trail you pass three signposted trail junctions on your right: for First Lake in about 10 minutes, then Dinkey Peak a couple of minutes later and finally the Dog Mountain Trail just before the parking lot. These destinations are described in hike #36, a good outing for another day.

# 38 ► Goldie and Flower Lakes

**Elevation gain:** 200 metres (650 feet)
**High point:** 960 metres (3,150 feet)
**Season:** July to October
**Topographical map:** Port Coquitlam 92G07
**Hiking time:** 2½ to 3 hours
Dog-friendly

This rewarding North Vancouver hike features a short (2-kilometre or 1¼-mile) climb through the forested slopes of Mount Seymour to explore two quite accessible yet serene little subalpine lakes. It takes you from the Deep Cove Lookout parking lot on Mount Seymour Road up the Perimeter Trail to the Goldie Lake and Flower Lake area. This hike is best done in midsummer to early fall, long after the snow melts and before the fall rains start, as these trails can be muddy and slippery in places at the best of times.

From Highway 1 in North Vancouver, take Exit 22 (Mount Seymour Parkway). Going east on Mount Seymour Parkway, turn left at Mount Seymour Road and proceed up to the Deep Cove Lookout parking lot just past the 8-kilometre signpost on Mount Seymour Road.

A couple of minutes in from the trailhead sign you reach a signposted junction with the Old Buck Trail, just past a footbridge over Allan Creek. Stay left here and proceed uphill on the old

Perimeter Trail. This trail is not a "walk in the park"; although just a short climb, it is rough and rugged, with lots of roots and rocks. In places it looks more like a streambed, but the frequent orange markers on the trees make it quite easy to follow.

About 25 to 35 minutes from the start you notice the Old Cabin Trail, from the Mount Seymour Group Campsite parking lot, coming in on your left. Just after this junction you take a foot-bridge across Scott-Goldie Creek, which originates up in the Flower Lake area. About 15 to 20 minutes later, you see a small lake on your left as you come to a signposted junction for the well-marked loop trails around both Goldie and Flower lakes.

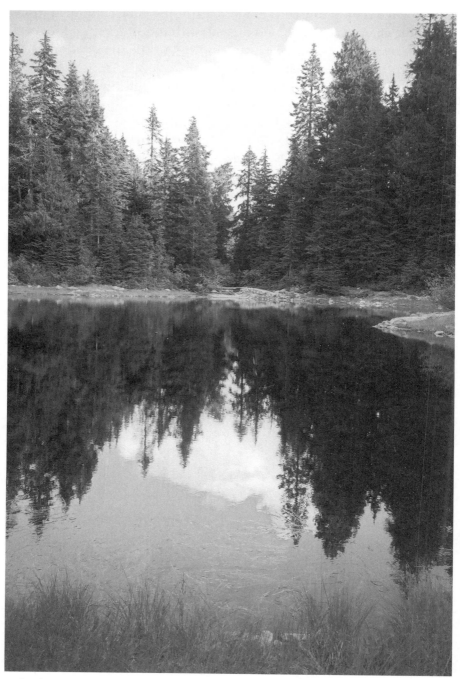

Looking west across Mount Seymour's Goldie Lake.

To first follow the Goldie Lake Loop, go right here, then right again at the next signpost about 25 metres (80 feet) ahead. The small lake on your left is not Goldie Lake; you reach it about 5 minutes farther along the somewhat rooty trail. Follow this trail counter-clockwise around Goldie Lake, about a 925-metre (half-mile) round trip taking 20 to 25 minutes. Along the way you find a nice, open, lakeside rest spot on the north side of the lake. Goldie is the better of the two lakes as the spot for a snack or lunch, and perhaps even a short swim on a hot day. After your break you are ready to explore Flower Lake, so continue on to the Flower Lake junction.

From the signposted junction follow the Flower Lake Loop trail to the southwest. You can make this 1.4-kilometre (.87-mile) round trip in 25 to 35 minutes. Like the Goldie Lake Loop this trail is easy to follow, but can be muddy in places. Flower Lake is smaller than Goldie Lake and quite reedy along the shoreline, without any obvious places for a rest stop.

Partway around Flower Lake there is a signposted junction for another short trail that branches off west toward the upper parking lot of Mount Seymour. This route is another possible starting point for a circuit of these two lakes, shorter and less strenuous, with little or no elevation gain. If you do start from this main parking area, look for the large "Goldie Meadows" sign just behind the washrooms building and follow the gravel path downhill, with the Goldie Rope Tow on your right. In less than 10 minutes and about 860 metres (a half mile) from the top you reach the signposted junction for the two lakes' loop trails. Later, signposts for the Ski Area Parking Lot will guide you back uphill.

Otherwise, returning from Flower Lake to the signposted Perimeter Trail junction, you now retrace your steps back downhill along the Perimeter Trail to the Deep Cove Lookout parking lot.

# 39 ▶ **Quarry Rock**

**Elevation gain:** 200 metres (650 feet)
**High point:** 220 metres (720 feet)
**Season:** Year-round
**Topographical map:** Port Coquitlam 92G07
**Hiking time:** 1½ to 2 hours
Dog-friendly

On this rewarding, all-season circuit, you venture out to a popular Deep Cove landmark and impressive viewpoint, with lots of ups and downs along the way to provide a little workout, and a variety of creeks and footbridges to keep it interesting. The hike takes you from the trailhead at Panorama Drive in North Vancouver northeast along the Baden-Powell (BP) Trail to Quarry Rock (sometimes referred to as Grey Rock), overlooking Deep Cove and Indian Arm.

From Highway 1 in North Vancouver, take either Exit 22 (Mount Seymour Parkway) or Exit 23 (Dollarton Highway). Follow the road east to Deep Cove Road, then stay on Deep Cove Road until it runs into Gallant Avenue in Deep Cove. Turn left onto Panorama Drive and park in the Panorama Park parking lot or as permitted by signs along Panorama Drive.

You begin at the signposted BP trailhead at the start of the 2500 block of Panorama Drive. This is also the eastern end of the annual Knee Knackering North Shore Trail Run, which follows the

48-kilometre (30-mile) BP Trail across the North Shore mountains from its western end near Horseshoe Bay. The trail is well marked with orange "BP" fleur-de-lis triangles on the trees. You first go up a flight of stairs then up a fairly steep stretch before the trail levels out a little.

About 15 minutes from the start you reach the fourth footbridge, signposted as Cove Creek, with wooden stairs on either side of it. Just a couple of minutes, or about 150 metres (490 feet), past Cove Creek there is a T-junction (marked with an orange "BP Trail" double-headed arrow on a tree to your left, and immediately opposite a massive old-growth District of North Vancouver-marked

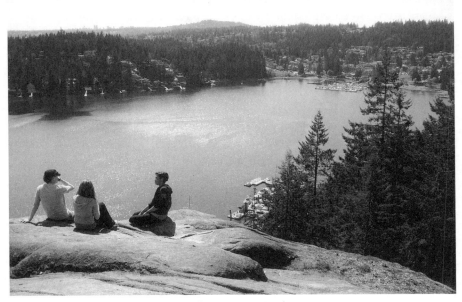

Looking back toward Deep Cove from Quarry Rock.

heritage Douglas fir just below you) with a connector trail leading up to Indian River Drive. You could continue straight ahead here to reach Quarry Rock in another 15 minutes or so, but turning up to the left gives you a little more elevation gain and a more interesting circle route approach to the Rock.

The trail is quite well worn and easy to follow, although not well marked other than by some occasional coloured flagging or metal squares on trees. After 10 to 15 minutes of fairly continuous uphill you reach Indian River Drive, where you turn right. A few metres ahead on the left there is a signposted junction with the BP Trail segment from Lynn Canyon to Deep Cove (see hike #20). Also, the trailhead for the rugged Three Chop Trail heading up Mount Seymour is on the other side of a nearby metal gate. You continue east on Indian River Drive for about 500 metres (one-third mile), passing under power lines just before reaching the signposted BP junction on your right. Take this trail downhill and back into the forest. In about 5 minutes you reach a wide, dirt road; continue straight ahead across the road to follow the BP downhill at the signpost. After another 5 minutes or so you come out at the power lines again. Continue south, directly across the open space and just to the right of the transmission tower, to pick up the BP as it heads downhill toward Quarry Rock.

In another couple of minutes you see your destination, the Quarry Rock bluff, in a clearing directly ahead of you. Rest for a while, enjoying the spectacular, 180-degree views of Deep Cove, Indian Arm and beyond. A hundred years ago Granite Quarries Ltd. was located just below this lookout and operated from 1908 to 1924. When you're ready to return, take the BP Trail to your left (west), rather than go back uphill the way you came in. At a steady pace you'll be back at the trailhead in a little over half an hour.

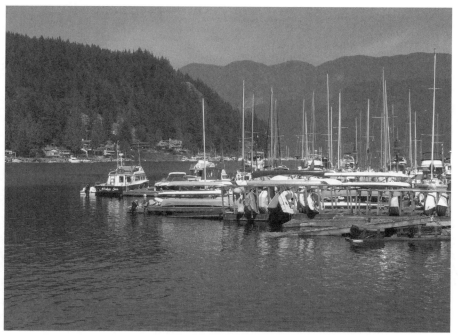

Quarry Rock (just above the left-most mast) from Panorama Park in Deep Cove.

# ADDENDUM

## Two Pemberton Area Hikes— Marriott Lake and Rohr Lake

Marriott Lake and Rohr Lake are worthy destinations if you are looking for an "Off the Beaten Path" hiking experience in the Pemberton area. Both lakes are in lovely settings, surrounded by mountain peaks and alpine meadows.

From Whistler, follow Highway 99 north toward Pemberton, turning right to go east through Mount Currie. The highway, now the Duffey Lake Road, takes you past Lillooet Lake, then quite steeply uphill through a series of switchbacks. About 20 kilometres (12½ miles) from Mount Currie, watch for the Joffre Lakes Provincial Park signs. Just 3½ kilometres (2.2 miles) past Joffre Lakes, you cross over Cayoosh Creek and almost immediately come to an unmarked junction with a gravel logging road on your left. If you are unable to turn left here, just over the next rise is a Ministry of Highways maintenance shed where you can turn around, then make a right-hand turn onto the gravel road. There are several pullouts for parking, but the road does become rough, with the type of vehicle you have determining how far up the road you can safely drive.

Follow the logging road north, staying left at a fork in the road, to reach the trailhead in 20 to 30 minutes, depending on where you parked. The trail is rough, steep in places, but quite well marked. About an hour in from the trailhead there is a signed junction where you stay left for Aspen Meadows/Marriott Lake or go right for Rohr Lake.

# Marriott Lake

**Elevation gain:** 400 metres (1,310 feet)
**High point:** 1,770 metres (5,800 feet)
**Season:** July to October
**Topographical map:** Duffey Lake 92J08
**Hiking time:** 4 to 6 hours, including lunch
Dog-friendly

An alpine hut, the Wendy Thompson Hut, built in 2000 by the Whistler section of the Alpine Club of Canada, is located just northwest of the lake at 1,755 metres (5,750 feet) elevation. Additional information, including a map and directions, can be found at Canadian Mountain Encyclopedia's bivouac.com using their Search feature, and entering "Wendy Thompson."

Looking east across Marriott Lake.

# Rohr Lake

**Elevation gain:** 430 metres (1,400 feet)
**High point:** 1,800 metres (5,900 feet)
**Season:** July to October
**Topographical map:** Duffey Lake 92J08
**Hiking time:** 4 to 6 hours, including lunch
Dog-friendly

Additional information on the Rohr Lake hike, including a map, photo and directions, can be found at the Simon Fraser University website: sfu.ca/geog351fall02/gp1/hiking/rohrlakeframeset.htm.

# Acknowledgements

Brochures for the Brothers Creek Forestry Heritage Walk and the Lawson Creek Forestry Heritage Walk were valuable information sources for several of the West Vancouver hikes, and can be obtained at the West Vancouver Museum and Archives in Gertrude Lawson House, 680 17th Street. Also, the Historical Photograph Collection of the West Vancouver Memorial Library, digital .westvanlibrary.ca, contains some remarkable photographs and historical information on the early days of West Vancouver.

The Hollyburn Heritage Society's website, hollyburnheritage. ca, and Francis Mansbridge's 2008 book *Hollyburn: The Mountain & The City* were both fascinating and comprehensive sources of historical information for the Hollyburn area.

Available at the West Vancouver Municipal Hall, 750 17th Street, is the West Vancouver District Map and Guide, with its excellent depiction of West Vancouver hiking trails. This map is also on the district's website at westvancouver.ca/dwv-maps/municipal-map/index.html.

BC Parks has an excellent map with the hiking trails in Cypress Provincial Park, available at env.gov.bc.ca/bcparks/explore/parkpgs/cypress/park_map.pdf.

The Friends of Cypress Provincial Park, cypresspark.ca, have also compiled and produced a new (as of July 2013), comprehensive and detailed hiking map of Cypress Provincial Park trails.

The Pacific Streamkeepers Federation website, Watershed Profiles section, pskf.ca/ecology/watershed/index.html, was also a valuable source of background information on the many creeks and rivers of North and West Vancouver.

The District of North Vancouver has two GIS Topography series maps on its website: Topography and Trails–Grouse Area and Topography and Trails–Seymour Area. They are available for free download at geoweb.dnv.org/maps. The maps are both very helpful references, although at time of writing the Seymour map did not yet include many of the trails that are featured in this book.

Metro Vancouver has maps available for areas such as the Lower Seymour Conservation Reserve (LSCR), Capilano River Regional Park and Lynn Headwaters Regional Park. These can be found at metrovancouver.org/about/maps/Pages/default.aspx and in brochure form at trailheads in the parks themselves.

In early 2006 the North Shore Mountain Bike Association (NSMBA), nsmba.ca, completed an extensive Seymour Trails Signpost Project, during which signposts with maps were installed at major intersections throughout the Seymour trail network. These signposts made travel along many of these trails much more user-friendly for the uninitiated. I personally found them invaluable as I was learning the trails, and would like to acknowledge the ongoing work of the NSMBA, which continues to improve our North Shore trails for the use of hikers and bikers alike.

Many thanks again to John Lightfoot of Lightfoot Art & Design Inc, whose many hours of meticulous work produced another amazing set of very detailed trail maps for this second edition.

I would also like to acknowledge Terry Peters, managing editor of the *North Shore News*, for agreeing to run my weekly hiking column in the newspaper during summer 2008 and again on their website, nsnews.com, during summer 2009. Erin McPhee carefully edited each one and managed the process on a weekly basis both years. Without having this reason in early 2008 to continue writing the hiking articles, I likely would never have reached the point of having enough to think about doing a book.

I also want to thank my editor Margaret Tessman, as well as Howard White, Anna Comfort O'Keeffe and all of the staff at Harbour Publishing for their dedication, hard work and support in helping make both the 2010 and 2014 editions of this book possible.

Finally, a major thank you to my dear friend Janet Bowyer, without whom this book would probably not have been written. From 2006 through 2013 Janet and her dog, Fritz, accompanied me more than once on all of these hikes, and many times on most of them. Janet thought of the "Off the Beaten Path" theme to initially help sell the idea of a hiking column to the *North Shore News* in spring 2008, then encouraged me to take the next big step of starting to work on the book that fall.